C000051633

The voice of

Theinspirationalseries™
Overcoming adversity and thriving

Geek Magnifique
Finding the Logic in my OCD
BY MELISSA BOYLE

We are proud to introduce The**inspirational**series™. Part of the Trigger family of innovative mental health books, The**inspirational**series™ tells the stories of the people who have battled and beaten mental health issues. For more information visit: www.triggerpublishing.com

THE AUTHOR

Melissa Boyle lives in Dorset, UK, with her husband and two cats. OCD has lurked in the corner of her mind for over 20 years, and she has also struggled with emetophobia (a fear of vomiting), a condition that's not very well known.

She is a journalist, mental health blogger, pizza aficionado, and unstoppable cat cuddler. She strongly believes that mental health needs an honest and open conversation, and wants to break down walls and end stigma. This inspired her to start blogging about her experiences on her site, *Geek Magnifique*.

Come and say hi to Melissa on Twitter: @geekmagnifique

First published in Great Britain 2018 by Trigger

Trigger is a trading style of Shaw Callaghan Ltd & Shaw Callaghan 23 USA, INC.

The Foundation Centre

Navigation House, 48 Millgate, Newark

Nottinghamshire NG24 4TS UK

www.triggerpublishing.com

Copyright © Melissa Boyle 2018

British Library Cataloguing in Publication Data

A CIP catalogue record for this book is available upon request
from the British Library

ISBN: 978-1-912478-01-9

This book is also available in the following e-Book and Audio formats:

MOBI: 978-1-912478-04-0
EPUB: 978-1-912478-02-6
PDF: 978-1-912478-03-3
AUDIO: 978-1-789561-03-6

Melissa Boyle has asserted her right under the Copyright,
Design and Patents Act 1988 to be identified as the author of this work

Cover design and typeset by Fusion Graphic Design Ltd

Printed and bound in Great Britain by Clays Ltd, Elcograf S.p.A

Paper from responsible sources

www.triggerpublishing.com

Thank you for purchasing this book.
You are making an incredible difference.

Proceeds from all Trigger books go directly to
The Shaw Mind Foundation, a global charity that focuses
entirely on mental health. To find out more about
The Shaw Mind Foundation visit,
www.shawmindfoundation.org

MISSION STATEMENT

Our goal is to make help and support available for every
single person in society, from all walks of life.
We will never stop offering hope. These are our promises.

Trigger and The Shaw Mind Foundation

A NOTE FROM THE SERIES EDITOR

The Inspirational range from Trigger brings you genuine stories about our authors' experiences with mental health problems.

Some of the stories in our Inspirational range will move you to tears. Some will make you laugh. Some will make you feel angry, or surprised, or uplifted. Hopefully they will all change the way you see mental health problems.

These are stories we can all relate to and engage with. Stories of people experiencing mental health difficulties and finding their own ways to overcome them with dignity, humour, perseverance and spirit.

Melissa's anxiety manifested itself in a fear of vomiting (emetophobia) which, when combined with her OCD, made her life challenging. On top of it all, she was struggling with the trauma from the abuse she suffered in her childhood, which had a tremendous impact on her life. Geek Magnifique shows how, through sheer determination, Melissa was able to reconcile her debilitating fear of germs with her fear of vomiting through tackling her anxiety. Her inspirational story proves that recovery is not an easy journey, but that it is an achievable one.

This is our Inspirational range. These are our stories. We hope you enjoy them. And most of all, we hope that they will educate and inspire you. That's what this range is all about.

Lauren Callaghan,
Co-founder and Lead Consultant Psychologist at Trigger

To B,

Thank you for giving me hope when I was at my lowest.
Thank you for showing me that my voice deserves to be heard.
Thank you for helping me to believe in myself again.
Thank you for loving me, even when I'm a pain in the arse.

Disclaimer: Some names and identifying details have been changed to protect the privacy of individuals.

Trigger Warning: This book contains references to sexual abuse, suicidal ideation, and graphic images of vomiting.

PROLOGUE

'One, two, three, four, five—'

A dog barked.

'One, two, three, four, five, six, seven—'

The toilet flushed. *Start again.*

'One, two, three, four, five—'

I'd been doing this for 20 minutes now. I was so tired and I just wanted to sleep, but it was important that I did this.

'One, two, three, four—'

I heard the loud *beeeep* of a car horn.

I started to feel hot and clammy with frustration, and I had a sick feeling in my stomach. It was like an itch under my skin that I just couldn't scratch. I *had* to get to 100 without any interruption. That's the only way this feeling would end, the only way my brain would let me rest.

By now I was sweating, my eyes filling with tears of frustration.

'One, two, three, four, five, six, seven, eight, nine ...'

I was going to get there this time, I could feel it.

'Ten, eleven, twelve, thirteen ...'

I started to tremble with a mix of emotions – frustration, anticipation, dread.

'Fourteen, fifteen—'

Another dog barked.

This time, I let out a wail of frustration. My mum came in and asked me what was wrong, but I didn't know what to say.

Why was I even doing this? The best way I can describe it now is that a fear of some sort of nameless, intangible, *bad* thing was driving me.

I was eight years old and fighting the same battle I faced every night at bedtime, a battle that made me dread going to sleep and beg my dad to read me just *one more story, please!*

But this was just the beginning, the start of a mental tug-of-war that would lead me down strange, dark, and difficult paths. Over the coming years, I would face struggles that would drag me through times of complete despair and hopelessness. By the time I reached adulthood, I would develop emetophobia – a debilitating fear of vomiting, one that would force me to go to increasingly extreme and dangerous lengths to avoid getting sick.

I didn't know it then, but my rituals would change over time, morphing into different demons that would taunt me at every turn. What I also didn't know was that these demons had a collective name: OCD.

CHAPTER 1

MELISSA BOYLE:
THE EARLY YEARS

I was a bit of an odd child – bright and intelligent at school, but prone to bursts of strong emotions and always niggled by feelings of unease.

The rituals quickly turned compulsive – like handwashing, for example. I would lather my hands with soap and plunge them under scalding hot water – and leave them there. I'd then refuse to touch things I thought were "dirty". I found a lot of things dirty.

The easiest way to explain contamination OCD is that it's as if your brain sees everything around you as a potential threat. And, unlike some brains that feel safe most of the time, yours is plagued by a constant sense of unease. It's like you've got a heightened sense of danger. If you don't know what that feels like, let me tell you – it's exhausting.

My relationship with my parents was always a little on the strained side. My dad worked from home, and so when I was really little, my mum decided that with nothing tying us down, we should travel the world. In many ways it was an enriching and privileged upbringing, but in many others, it was unsettled and lonely.

We lived in some incredible places including Fiji, New Zealand, the south of France and Montserrat. I had the chance to experience amazing cultures, meet interesting people, and see ways of life that humbled and inspired me.

But I felt isolated and rootless. I never had the chance to make any real friends or have somewhere I could call home. My mum used to tell this story about a time when we were on a long-haul flight and I woke up confused about where we were. I didn't know what time it was, whether it was night or day, or if we were coming or going. She laughed about it; it was supposed to be a cute little anecdote, but now when I think about it, I just feel sad.

We eventually came back to England when I was about seven or eight, and rented a small house in Northants. Initially it was just me and my dad, while my mum tied up the loose ends back in France. It was strange when it was just the two of us, but nice in some ways. I enjoyed a slightly more relaxed atmosphere, without some of the usual pressures my mum put on me – for example, extra maths lessons at home with her, or memory training. I made friends with our elderly next-door neighbour, and sort of felt like a normal kid.

For a little while my dad worked in an office and I would visit him on the evenings he had to stay late. I'd enjoy running around, looking at all the books, and playing in the rolling stacks. Eventually my mum joined us, and we were able to buy a house in a nearby town.

I think the move was really good for me. I adored my new school, I made some good friends, and I started karate lessons. I loved our house because I had a really big bedroom, and we adopted a couple of cats, Boris and Hercules. We spent a couple of really happy years there and we reconnected with extended family. I felt like I was starting to have all the trappings of a regular, happy childhood.

But, of course, this was when my OCD really started. And as I became more and more stressed and unhappy, it was decided that what I needed was a "fresh start" in a new town. I was devastated. It didn't feel at all like what I needed, but rather what my parents wanted. As an adult, I can see that what I probably needed was professional help.

In 1998 we moved again, and I didn't like the town at first. Our house wasn't very nice; the previous owners had decorated it in garish shades of lime green and orange, and there wasn't a garden. Unlike our last home which was in a nice, quiet cul-de-sac, our new house was on an ugly road of terraced houses. I had trouble sleeping, not just because of my night-time rituals, but because of the colony of seagulls that lived on our roof and insisted on squawking during all hours of the sodding day and night.

Once again, I found myself starting from scratch, with a new school and no friends. As always, though, I managed to settle in, and when the time came for me to start secondary school, I felt quite excited – everyone would be in the same boat as me: new and nervous.

I was always pushed hard to do well in school, which I'm grateful for. In many ways, however, I felt like I wasn't allowed to be a child. Whether it's because I was an only child, or because my parents just wanted me to be mature, it seemed to me like anything "childish" was looked upon with derision.

Crying was referred to as "whinging", and I was shrugged off for being too sensitive. My mother encouraged my bedrooms to have grown-up décor, such as muted colours and hardwood floors. Cartoons were often shunned in favour of more serious movies, and in many ways, I never felt like I could just be silly. I was expected to see the world – and approach it – like an adult.

It's hard to put into words, but I feel like I was always expected to be wise beyond my years. When we were house-hunting (I would have probably been about nine years old), an estate agent asked me what my must-have things would be. I said all the things I'd heard my parents mention – a garage, garden, three bedrooms, and two bathrooms – but afterwards my mother scoffed and said it was silly to expect all of that. I felt silly and embarrassed but didn't say anything about it. Did she expect me to understand how the housing market worked and what was realistic for our budget? To be honest, considering I was nine, I feel like my mother should have been glad I didn't ask for a slide instead of stairs and a paddock for my unicorns.

I used to take part in Kumon, an after-school maths programme (so cool, right?). I remember doing an open day so people could watch how it worked, during which we had to solve maths problems within a time limit. The idea was for us to work our way through a standard booklet of homework sums, but as quickly as we could, in order to demonstrate the skills we'd learnt. Now I think about, it's rather bizarre. Doing sums is hardly a spectator sport, and I can't imagine what would possess someone to stop and watch.

I was on something like Level H at this point (doing fractions and more complicated stuff), but for the open day I just wanted to do some easy work. I was doing this stupid maths thing on a Saturday instead of having fun with my friends, and I'm pretty sure I didn't want to be there. My mum, seeing me working on the easy level, told me off and said with a sneer, 'People will think you're retarded.'

I immediately felt ashamed and inadequate. Thankfully, I don't think anybody heard.

If I had any goals she didn't think were worthwhile (like wanting to win a medal at sports day), I would often be made to feel unsupported and silly for wanting something so trivial.

I think the pressure and lack of approval I experienced have made me a lot harder on myself. Even now, I feel embarrassed if I show too much emotion. I apologise constantly for the smallest things and have a desperate need to please people. At times I have an almost excruciating fear of upsetting or offending others. I always seek reassurance that the people in my life still love me, because I'm afraid that the smallest thing I've said will have ruined our relationship.

I believe my relationship with my parents is a huge contributing factor to my overall mental state, and this is something that I ended up exploring in great detail along my road to recovery.

If you cut yourself and see blood, your nervous system responds by triggering a physical sensation of pain. You don't sit there telling yourself that you're fine; you put a plaster on the cut and care for it until it's healed. You don't have an angry voice in your head telling you that it's all your fault, or that something terrible will happen if you put a stop to your pain.

But *mental* illness often does the opposite. It tells you that the pain is your fault, that putting a stop to it (for example, by cutting short a cycle of obsessive compulsions) will make bad things happen. It tricks you into thinking that you're fine, even when all the signs are pointing the opposite way.

It took me a long time to get the courage to pull at those threads and begin unravelling myself so I could put myself back together again.

Out of all the many roads my damaged little mind has led me down, the most important one has been recovery. There were times when I felt broken beyond repair, but over time I sought help and slowly, slowly began to win more of the daily battles against my brain.

I reclaimed the person I knew was buried inside me, brushed the dust off her clothes, and showed her that things could be different. Things could be *better*.

This tale of mine isn't supposed to make you fear mental illness. If you have similar struggles with your own demons, let this be a message of hope. If you're struggling right now, I hope that my story gives you a bit of courage and helps to show you that there's light at the end of the tunnel.

If you keep turning these pages, what I can promise you in return is honesty, inspiration (while that's so corny I almost made myself sick, the fact that I'm even joking about being sick is actually inspiring in itself), and hopefully a couple of laughs along the way.

Ready?

Let's get our combs and brush out the knots in my ridiculous little brain. Let's delve into its nonsense and try to make some sense of it all. Let's sift through the irrational thoughts and try to find logic in the illogical.

CHAPTER 2

THE MAN WHO CHANGED ME

I was eight years old when a family friend began acting inappropriately towards me. It started out with him saying suggestive things to me. He told me I "excited" him. I knew instinctively that it wasn't a normal thing to say, but I was too young to really understand what it meant. Like my little niggling brain demons, inappropriate words soon morphed and changed into something much uglier. Suggestive talk turned to touching.

I started dreading being on my own with him. We would play tennis together, usually with my dad, unless he was too busy. On the days he was, I remember crying, pretending to be ill, and finding other excuses not to play.

At some point when I was a bit older, he came to visit us. He took a lot of photos of me, I seem to remember, and made comments about my looks. Something about those comments didn't sit right with me. They felt more like something a lover would say, rather than a family friend.

When he took me to the beach one day and casually slipped his hand down my top to cup my breast, I felt numb. I wasn't afraid, sad or angry, I just *was*. As he squeezed my breast with his large, weathered hand, I'm sure I heard him moan softly.

He did it so openly and brazenly that there was a part of me that wasn't even sure he was doing anything wrong. He stayed there for probably around 15 seconds, saying nothing.

Afterwards he told me not to tell anyone about what he'd done, because it would upset my parents and he'd go to jail. It sounds so textbook, doesn't it? On the way home, he bought me a Britney Spears CD.

On my 13th birthday we went to his flat and my parents popped out to buy me a cake. I remember he said something about me being a woman now, and then he made me kiss him. His hands, though they stayed above my clothes, wandered lower than they had done in the past.

I think that was the first time I properly felt afraid of him. I remember his musky smell, his big, rough hands, and the bristle of his stubble against my face, which was smooth and still slightly rounded by puppy fat. I could no longer ignore that this was wrong. Everything about it felt unnatural and made my insides clench and my nerve endings itch.

The abuse was no longer passive. I couldn't just sit and ignore it while he touched me; he *made* me kiss him. I hadn't wanted to – I think I'd even pulled away – but he forced me to kiss him on the lips.

That night, I knew I had to tell my parents. I'd just unwrapped one of my birthday presents from a school friend – a little dolphin toy that I was lying in bed and playing with. It had been a difficult day. I'd cried a lot, picked fights with my parents, and pretty much sabotaged my own birthday. The weird thing is, at this point, I don't even think I told them about the abuse so it would stop; I think I just wanted them to understand why I'd been so difficult all day.

I didn't call them upstairs. Instead, I lay there crying loudly enough for them to hear me. When they came and sat at the foot of my bed, it was so hard to get the words out.

Do you ever talk to someone and find yourself wondering what the other person would do if you suddenly said something really rude to them for no reason? It's impossible to imagine their reaction, because it's simply a situation you'd never find yourself in. That's what this felt like. I had no idea how they'd react.

I don't remember what I said, but I distinctly remember my mother going downstairs and throwing up violently. I then heard her phone him to tell him never to contact us again. My father, always calm and stoic, said very little and let my mother take charge.

The strange thing is that, even though I knew objectively that what he was doing was wrong, once I knew it was over I had a hard time making myself feel anything. It was almost as if I knew I was supposed to feel upset or outraged, but deep down I couldn't quite make myself believe I was. I just felt nothing. In the same way you might poke a bruise to see if it hurts, I would think about what he did and try to measure my response. Whatever little emotion I could drum up felt forced, so I locked what happened away, for fear of learning something about myself I didn't want to – that I wasn't like other people. I was afraid that I was somehow cold or broken inside, and I didn't want to think about what that meant about me as a person.

CHAPTER 3

REPEAT AFTER ME: PHOBIAS AREN'T RATIONAL

You're still with me? Thank goodness! You probably deserve a beer or something for staying with me, so go and grab one – I'll wait.

Sorted? Alright then, onwards we go.

There's a very good chance you bought this book (huge thank you for that, by the way!) because it talks about emetophobia. Perhaps it's something you've experienced, or perhaps you know someone who is going through it and you want to understand them a little better.

Emetophobia, or the fear of vomiting, is, quite frankly, a horrible thing to live with.

Frustratingly, as you may well know, telling your loved ones you have emetophobia is often met with one of three responses:

1. 'Oh, I have that too.'

   Of course, that could certainly be true, but in my experience, people are very often hyperbolic when it comes to their dislike of vomiting. There's a genuine difference between not liking it (who does?!) and having a crippling fear of it that leaves you unable to feed yourself or sometimes even leave the house.

2. 'But no one *likes* being sick.'

   Yes, obviously. As I've already said, who does?! But again,

there's a big, gargantuan difference between not liking something and having a fear that completely consumes and controls your life.

3. 'Being sick is a natural thing / the body doing what it needs to do / won't kill you ...' or some other crappy platitude that you rationally know to be true but that *doesn't matter because phobias aren't rational! Aaaaaaaaaaaaaaaaaaaaaaaaaaaaaargh!*

I know that last one shouldn't frustrate me as much as it does because people are only ever trying to help, but it upsets me because of course I know it's true. *Of course* I know all of those things, but there is no magic way to make me believe them. I'm not frustrated at any of those well-meaning people, I'm frustrated at myself. Why can't I see the world like they do – rationally and logically?

Because, once again, mental illness is a sneaky little son of a biscuit, one that uses lies and trickery to get what it wants – which, in my case, was to live in some sort of permanent state of high alert. I had a nice little bit of fear simmering away in the pit of my stomach, prickling my skin and making me hyperaware of everything I ate, touched, and even said.

Cheers, brain, that's great. Really super.

I was always hyperaware of the things I said, because there's also a fun little added superstitious element to emetophobia. Some emetophobes won't even say any words pertaining to being sick, out of fear that it will somehow actually make them sick. At one point, I couldn't say or write the word "norovirus" in case the word somehow came to life and infected me. Ridiculous really, isn't it?

Sometimes I would try to bolster my confidence by telling myself, 'I'm not going to be sick.' This, to me, was tempting fate, and meant I had to knock on wood five times. Always five – I don't know why.

Despite this, I'm not a particularly superstitious person by nature, and I'm aware of how illogical it is to be afraid of words.

So, once again, the most frustrating thing about this whole situation was myself. Why couldn't I shut off those ridiculous, irrational thoughts?

The first time that I can clearly remember experiencing the all-consuming panic of emetophobia was when I was around 16 or 17 and sitting on my parents' sofa. I was hyperventilating because I felt sick. The same thought kept going through my head, over and over:

You can't be sick. This can't happen.

I don't remember much else of how I was feeling; I just remember having this deep and overwhelming panic. I knew I was going to be sick, but I didn't know exactly when. There was no stopping it; I simply had to let my body do what it needed to. I had no control over the situation, and that frightened me.

My mum came into the room to find me in a complete state of terror, and asked me if I needed to go to the hospital. I don't suppose she'd ever seen me like that before. I was eventually sick later that night. I squeezed my eyes shut while it was happening so that I wouldn't have to see anything, and tried not to breathe too much through my nose. Tears sprung out from under my eyelids reflexively, and I giggled shakily due to the adrenaline wearing off.

Once the evidence was flushed and I'd cleaned myself up, I felt an overwhelming rush of relief that the whole thing was over. My body had done what it needed to do and I had no more nausea. That was of little comfort to me, though. You know how women forget the pain of childbirth as nature's way of stopping them from being too afraid to go through it all again? Well, emetophobia does the opposite. It forgets how much better you feel after being sick, instead fixating on every unpleasant moment of the act itself.

The back of my throat burnt with bile and I felt a little unsteady on my feet. I guess I was shaken up from the intense panic I'd experienced not that long ago.

After I'd calmed down, I admitted my phobia to my mum. It was probably the first time I'd said it out loud.

'I've never seen you so worked up,' she told me, with concern and confusion lacing her words.

'Well,' I started nervously, 'I get really worried when I think I'm going to throw up. I think I'm afraid of it happening.' I struggled to find the right words to vocalise what had only been an instinctive, subconscious feeling up until then.

'I wish I'd known. I had no idea.'

Yeah, you and me both, Mum. I don't think I fully knew until that night either.

That's what strikes me as odd when I look back on it now: that I told her this like it was something I'd consciously thought about before. Maybe on some level I'd previously felt a sense of fear at the thought of vomiting, but it was nothing compared to the panic I felt that night.

If I really think about it, I can remember times when I couldn't sleep because I felt a bit queasy and anxious. But something definitely changed on the sofa that night, because that fear was intense, real, and visceral; it was like nothing I'd experienced before.

Whatever the reason, my phobia decided to kick itself up a notch (or 10) from then on, and I couldn't have imagined how much it would come to control my life.

CHAPTER 4

FALLING IN LOVE (AND OFF ROOFS)

Emetophobia continued to lurk menacingly in the crevices of my mind long after the night of my pre-puke panic attack.

When I was 18 I went to university in Winchester. I was fortunate to take this massive step with my two best friends, who are like sisters to me. As someone who never really laid down any roots, I've known for many years that having "old" friends – and sharing a history with people – is unbelievably special. This pair were Sarah – my wonderful friend that fate (or the alphabet – our surnames both began with "W", so we were put next to each other in science class and the rest, as they say, is history) brought into my life – and Julie, who entered slightly later, but whose path has been closely intertwined with mine ever since.

On my second day at university, I met a boy called Dave. We were put into the same house in the student village. It wasn't the cutest of first meetings ...

The night before, on what was his first night as a university student, he'd had a few drinks and decided it would be a brilliant idea to climb onto the corrugated metal roof covering our porch. Because, why not? And also, alcohol.

With someone equally as intoxicated giving him a boost, he managed to sort of half-scrabble, half-crawl his way onto the roof. All was going well (sort of), until he realised that there was nothing for him to grab hold of because, well, it was a metal roof and wasn't designed for being climbed on by drunk teenagers. As he started to slide back, he realised two things:

- The person spotting him was going to be of little to no use
- If he was to avoid breaking anything, he was going to need to slow down his descent, which meant ...

Slice. His hands flew out and grabbed the first thing they could, which just so happened to be the edge of the metal roof. The very sharp edge of the metal roof.

Immediate threat of broken limbs averted, he carefully lowered himself back down to the ground and inspected the damage to his hand. Sure enough, two of his fingers had deep, bleeding gashes.

And that's why, the next morning, I was greeted by the sight of our other housemate, Danny, mopping blood off the front porch while Dave waved at me sheepishly with his bandaged hand.

What followed that awkward moment was a series of even more awkward ones. We made small talk over the cup of tea he was too polite to decline (I later found out he hates tea!) and bonded over our freshers' nerves, sharing stories from home. After our little kitchen chats I would run upstairs to chat to my friend Nada on MSN Messenger (sheesh, who else remembers that?) and tell her all about the cute boy I'd met. I know – I couldn't have been more of a cliché if I'd tried!

The start of our relationship was sweet but often rocky. There was a lot of uncertainty and more than a few arguments for the first year or so, even though we loved each other. I grew attached very quickly, while it took Dave a little longer to get to the "serious commitment" stage. It's completely understandable when I look back on it now, but at the time it was a little bit too much for my teenage heart to take. I took every request for space as a sign that our relationship was failing. I would spend those periods of time that we spent apart crying, feeling sick, and desperately seeking reassurance from my friends. But from very early on in our relationship there was something about him that made me feel safe. I opened up to him about my childhood trauma after a few months of being together because I knew instinctively that I could trust him. We didn't really talk about my mental illness because I still didn't really understand it or let myself believe that I had a problem.

We laughed and cried, made up stupid dances, had melodramatic fights, taught ourselves to make sushi, and ate a lot of baked Camembert together.

One of the many weird things about emetophobia is that sufferers are very rarely sick. No one is completely sure whether the fear somehow prevents the vomiting, or if the rarity of vomiting creates the sense of fear. I was sick a few times at university – more frequently than I was used to, to be honest. Two of those times were alcohol related (oops), and the drunkenness somehow numbed any feelings of panic.

I was, however, sick once when I was sober, and the panic came back. I remember asking Dave why this was happening to me. He told me he didn't know, but suggested a few possible reasons, such as dehydration and heatstroke. But I wasn't satisfied. I didn't like how random it felt – I hadn't eaten anything weird and I hadn't been around anyone with a bug. As my mind frantically tried to find an explanation, I started to realise it was the lack of control that I hated. I didn't like how my body could suddenly take over, and I didn't like that there was no way to stop it once it started. This made sense to me, but it wasn't exactly comforting. Being afraid of a lack of control is like fearing *fear* itself; it's a vicious cycle, a menacing beast that feeds off you to sustain itself.

Now, I know you probably aren't reading this for a detailed chronicle of all the times I've been sick. But I'm meandering towards a point, I promise!

For the most part, my emetophobia was manageable during this time. Yes, there was always a slight fear nagging me from the very back of my brain, but it wasn't controlling me as such. I knew my limits alcohol-wise, and I was careful not to overstep them, but unlike some emetophobes I was perfectly comfortable clubbing, getting drunk, and socialising with drunk people (something that happened a lot at uni, though thankfully without too many incidences of vomiting). Being around drunk people wasn't scary to me because if they got sick, it wasn't like I could catch something from them. I just didn't find the idea of seeing them vomit too appealing.

I wasn't particularly careful about what I ate – or at least, I took no more than the standard precautions you'd expect a reasonable person to take. I even handled and cooked raw chicken, something which became impossible for me to even fathom later on.

It's hard to pinpoint exactly when I started to develop more and more of what my therapist would later term my "safety behaviours". I would come to learn that these were all the habits I'd adopted to keep myself "safe", in line with the standards set by my OCD and emetophobia. Such behaviours included excessive handwashing, avoidance of certain foods, and reluctance to use public bathrooms.

These behaviours grew more and more extreme over time, until they reached a head some years later.

Growing up, my mother and I clashed terribly. I always felt weak and silly around her, and I found her harsh and abrasive. There was no such thing as winning an argument with her; she would simply shout louder than I could, or ignore me. I hated fighting with her. Something about her demeanour and how she refused to see things from my point of view absolutely infuriated me. I once got so angry at her during one of our fights that I threw a big bottle of fizzy drink at her. It wobbled through the air and dropped like a lead balloon barely two feet away from me, so it's not quite as dramatic as it sounds. I'm not proud of it, and I can't explain why, but no one has ever angered me quite the way she could.

It seemed like nothing was ever good enough for her, and if she felt like I had wronged her in any way, she wouldn't let me forget it. I once bought her a Mother's Day card and a box of chocolates I knew she liked, and for some reason (I think possibly because the card wasn't handmade) she pretended she hadn't seen them on the table next to her. It wasn't until I pointed them out that she gave them a quick, dismissive glance and an insincere 'that's nice'.

I always felt much closer to my dad, but as I got older it began to frustrate me that he would always take her side.

After I left home for university, I started to notice unusual shifts in her behaviour. She had suffered from chronic back pain since I was a child, and by this point she was barely leaving the house. She never seemed to have any friends, and with my dad working from home, they gradually shut themselves away.

I would speak to my parents fairly regularly on the phone, and I noticed that my mother started believing some unusual things. She thought that the government was trying to poison us by spraying chemicals from planes and that the "elite" were reptilian aliens. She believed in false flag operations and government conspiracies, and thought that everyone in the world was out to get her.

I played it down as her being a bit quirky – perhaps it was a hormonal thing, or some sort of strange manifestation of empty nest syndrome. But it wasn't long before her beliefs and her attitude towards me began to seriously affect our relationship.

By the end of university, Dave and I were solid. We'd spent time with each other's families and I'd had a wonderful time showing him my home town, where we played chess in my bedroom at my parents' house, went on lovely walks, and had a disastrously windy picnic at Camber Sands.

On the day I got my university results, Dave and I were at the house, celebrating and telling Mum how excited we were about graduation. She began looking at the skies and sighing dramatically as another plane flew by, "spraying chemicals". I asked her if, for that one day, we could just be happy and forget about all of that, at which point she shouted that I was selfish, that there were more important things to think about than a stupid graduation ceremony where I'd have to go up on stage wearing "satanic robes" (don't ask – I have no idea).

I was devastated and went back up to my room feeling dejected and ashamed. I could hear my dad telling her to "just let me enjoy my moment"; I think this was the one and only time I ever heard him stand up to her for me.

When it came to deciding what to do after university, we chose to move in with Dave's family in Dorset. I had never really imagined myself going back to my home town, and though it was incredibly tough to leave my two best friends behind, I was excited about starting a new adventure.

Dave and I soon moved into a flat with his close friend, Pete, and I went back to university to retrain to be a solicitor – a classic "Help, I can't find a job!" panic move. If I'm being honest with myself, I chose law for all the wrong reasons. I had a very romanticised view of what being a lawyer would be like, and got swept up by the appeal of having an impressive, high-status job. Sadly – but perhaps not surprisingly, given my reasons for pursuing it – my law career ended as quickly as it started. I *just* scraped a pass, and did not become a solicitor. My mother mightily disapproved of me studying law, claiming that I was going to become a part of the "corrupt" legal system. It was while I was studying that our relationship hit the first of many large hurdles.

Though I was no closer to knowing what I wanted to do career wise, when Dave took me to the top of the London Eye and asked me to marry him – well, I knew I wanted to do that!

After Dave and I got engaged, we went to visit my parents to tell them the good news. They seemed completely disinterested to me. There were no questions – not an ounce of visible excitement – and I practically had to thrust the ring in my mother's face so that she would look at it. Again, I was left feeling silly for showing any signs of happiness about something my mother didn't find significant.

I persevered, though, and made plans to bring Dave back to spend Christmas with them. We talked about it and everything was arranged. I was so excited.

Then, September came and I forgot to send my mum a birthday card. I called her on her birthday to apologise and wish her a happy birthday, sent her an e-card and posted a real card to her too. I thought things were fine.

Nearer to Christmas I emailed to confirm the plans for coming home.

I received a reply stating, in no uncertain terms, that they didn't want to make any plans with me that Christmas, and suggested that maybe I could visit them at Easter instead. Dad also told me that Mum was upset because she hadn't received any communication from me all year, and that she was particularly hurt when she hadn't received a birthday card. He told me that I had to repair some bridges with her.

I was stunned. I rang Dave up from the university library, crying. Eventually, when I felt a bit more composed, I replied. Perhaps I was a little on the aggressive side, but I was so hurt. And so, so angry.

I wanted to say that I'm sorry that I have been somewhat absent recently. I've let myself get snowed under a bit with uni and making new friends, and I haven't been the best at keeping in touch.

But I would like to defend myself and say that it hasn't been easy for me at all. Things are a lot better now, but it wasn't that long ago that I really didn't enjoy talking to you guys as much. How could I, when all you would talk about was the end of the world, reptilian aliens, chemtrails, and so much more, so that I would be begging you to stop?

On the day I got my university results, you made it quite clear you didn't give a crap. You even told me I was selfish for wanting to celebrate. Do you have any idea how crap that made me feel?

You never once said you were proud of me. Mum, you haven't shown any real interest in my course (not you, Dad, you have, and

I'm really grateful for all the articles and books you've sent me). You have no real idea what I'm doing, or how hard it is, or how crap it makes me feel that, now I finally have direction, you still don't seem to be proud of me, or even care. I honestly don't know what would make you proud. Dave's mum raves to everyone who will listen that he has a degree.

I'm sorry for not sending a birthday card, but you don't even write in cards to me, Mum. You get Dad to write the messages. And all your emails that say "email me, I miss you"? Why don't you email me? Or phone me?

I never mean to make you feel like a hotel, but I have to say you haven't always made it easy when I come back. I used to love bringing friends round to have dinner all together, but now you won't allow me to have friends at the house. That would be the easiest way of seeing everyone, but that doesn't work for you. You have no idea how hard it is being away from my friends, how much of a pull there is on me, and how many people I have to please.

But I had such a good time when we came back JUST TO SEE YOU, and I felt things were really good again. I know I haven't expressed it as much as I should, but I have been really homesick, and maybe I should have told you that more. But I'd have thought that when I cry when we leave, you would see that. And then to hear that you don't want me to come home at all till Easter, well that was the most hurtful thing you could have said.

But what's worse about Christmas is that I don't care about doing anything special. It didn't have to be lavish or expensive, it just meant so much to me to bring Dave back for our first Christmas together with you. It took me ages to arrange coming back for Christmas, and it meant so much to me. I've always said that it meant a lot to me, and not to see my friends, or for any other reason, but to spend Christmas day with Dave for the very first time, with you as a family.

What's worse is that I know you won't take this in, or see my point of view at all. I honestly wanted to apologise, but I also felt I had to express myself. Dad thinks I have bridges to rebuild, which I will, but maybe you could look at how you've been making me feel.

I feel like a reasonable person would look at that email and maybe think, *shit, maybe I'm a little bit in the wrong too.* Someone with a tiny bit of empathy would perhaps see that I was struggling.

But Dad responded again, telling me that society had to be aware of the potential dangers it is facing, such as vaccinations and chemtrails, suggesting that I do my own research and come to my own conclusions. He also insisted that Mum was within her rights to be horrified about how much money I'd spent on my graduation, considering how others are struggling financially. He then told me that although Mum was, in fact, very proud of me, as an adult I shouldn't need their validation. I should have been grateful, according to him, that Mum cared so much about me, and it was childish of me to expect her to rack up a giant telephone bill after I'd not responded to their emails.

I guess I saw that coming, didn't I? As always, they completely and deliberately misunderstood or ignored everything I said, and instead tried to disarm me with garbled conspiracy theories, ridiculous accusations, and pseudo-science.

This was my response:

Firstly, I wasn't talking about the celebrating, I was talking about when Mum started talking about chemtrails when I got my results, and I asked if for just a while, we could talk about me and my achievement, and she said I was being selfish.

I know I'm not a child, but that doesn't mean it isn't nice to hear that you're proud. Talking about graduation gowns being "robes of Satan", and the English legal system being a farce doesn't exactly sound like pride to me.

I meant that in general Mum could phone or email. And I have said many times if you ring my mobile and hang up I will call you back. That doesn't run up a massive phone bill.

You didn't mention Christmas at all. Am I to understand that you are standing firm on this despite what I said? It really makes me sad that you would throw this away after everything I said and how special I wanted it to be with all of us. You have no idea how much Christmas meant to me, both spending it with you and bringing Dave home. It's been the plan all year, and suddenly you're taking it away. I really resent being told to grow up when I'm just telling you how I feel.

I won't beg you, but I really want to make things right, and have a special (but relaxed and cheap Christmas). If you really don't want to see me, then that's your choice, but I want to be the grown-up and just put this behind us, and spend Christmas with my boyfriend and my family.

If you really can't put yourself out to see me for a few days, then I don't really know what to say to that.

Perhaps now they'd see how hurt I was.

Like bollocks they did! All they told me was that neither of them was up for coping with visitors, and that they would quietly do their own thing, giving everyone time for reflection.

I tried a few more times to basically beg them to change their minds. I apologised for making Mum feel bad and told them that I'd been deeply hurt too. I said a number of times that I just wanted to move on. I told them that I loved them and really wanted to spend Christmas with them, and apologised again. There were a few more emails back and forth, but I knew I was fighting a losing battle, clinging onto some sort of desperate hope. But with one final email from Dad – stating that they wanted to be on their own and just forget about Christmas altogether – the discussion was over.

We didn't spend Christmas with them that year, and I had the complete and utter humiliation of having to tell Dave's family that the plans had changed because my parents had decided they no longer wanted to spend Christmas with me.

I never ended up spending another Christmas with them again.

I probably should have realised then that our relationship was over, that I was only going to keep getting hurt. But I kept fighting, thinking things would change.

The sad thing is, we're not so dissimilar, my mother and I. Like me, she is afraid of the world around her – it's just that her fear manifests itself in shadowy government organisations and sinister plots, rather than stomach bugs and dirt.

We reconciled after that awful Christmas, but things felt different and I could no longer really enjoy spending time with my parents.

My failed foray into the legal world was quickly followed by a glamorous role in insurance, and it was during this job that I decided I wanted to become an events co-ordinator. I was planning my own wedding at the time, and the idea of helping others do the same was really appealing. Pete was working at the Marriott Hotel, and he would tell me a bit about what it was like being a hotel events co-ordinator.

With his help, I got a job in the Conference and Banqueting department there, which is basically the operations team that looks after all the events on the day. It involved a lot of crazy hours, moving tables, and serving food, but since it was going to get me my coveted events role, I didn't mind too much.

Looking back, I find it find very strange that I was so relaxed about food around that time. When we were on shift, our meals were typically the guests' leftovers – meat that had been sitting on a buffet table, chicken left under a heat lamp, cheese and other dairy items that had been left out of the fridge – and it seems crazy to me that I ate these things. Perhaps it helped knowing that everyone else was eating the same food, and that it had been prepared by a highly skilled chef.

Weirdly, it was a risotto that one of the chefs made specifically for me that sent me into a spiralling panic, what with the reheated rice and all that. I was worried that it had been sitting around for ages and would make me sick. I spent ages trying to recall the sensation of the rice in my mouth – was it hot? Were the flavours more sour than usual?

Funny how these things work, right? Not "haha" funny, of course, because there's nothing enjoyable about sneaking off to the toilets to panic Google (can I coin the term "poogling"?) food poisoning statistics and read horror stories from other rice eaters. But it was "strange and bizarre" funny.

My hard work, rice-Googling, and unsociable hours paid off, and I quickly moved into an office-based events role. It was here where my emetophobia came to a crippling head. That winter in 2012 was the worst one I'd ever experienced. The norovirus dominated the headlines that year; the papers were full of scaremongering stories about the thousands of people whose Christmas would be ruined by the bug, and there were warnings every other day about places to avoid, along with constant reminders about hand hygiene.

The relaxed, laissez-faire attitude I'd cultivated in my last job (excluding the occasional freak out, of course) was slowly fading away, and I was reaching a point where I was becoming hyperaware of everything I touched and ate. The constant stomach bug warnings sent my mind spiralling even more.

How did I go from a devil-may-care, room-temperature-leftover-eater to someone who would microwave the shit out of everything and was suddenly too good to eat old, shrivelled quiche? (I know – who did I think I was, the Queen?)

I have no idea. It might have been that my phobia had grown more intense so my brain started tricking me into believing more and more things were unsafe. I had a bit of a scare and it really knocked my confidence. I helped myself to lunch in the staff kitchen – vegetables, potatoes, and gravy – but didn't bother to heat it up. The moment I'd eaten the last bite, I panicked. That gravy was made with meat juice, and it had been sitting under a heat lamp for goodness knows how long. I'd just plunged a ladle into a greasy brown swamp full of bacteria and slurped up every last drop. *Shit.*

I spent a near-hysterical 15 minutes in the bathroom poogling food safety advice and texting a chef friend for their opinion. The general consensus was that I'd be fine, but I didn't listen to that – instead I listened to the two or three horror stories of gastrointestinal mutiny. As always, I was completely fine, but I still spent a nervous 12 hours over-analysing every stomach gurgle and counterproductively making myself queasy with anxiety.

Over those months I would lie awake at night, imagining the sensation of being sick over and over again, until I'd worked myself into a tearful panic. I analysed every feeling or twinge in my body, searching for signs of stomach upset.

With constant reports of norovirus outbreaks, work became a nightmare. Hotels, just like cruise ships, are the sort of place where bugs can spread like wildfire. Management was very aware of the risks and posted signs everywhere, reminding staff to practise good hygiene. Pump bottles of Purell popped up on every desk, and it felt like every day someone in the office was talking about a friend or family member who'd been struck down by "Nora".

If I'd been on high alert before, my paranoia was now reaching dangerous levels. The intrusive thoughts in my head were screaming like an air raid siren. My dull, lingering fear became a burning, all-consuming terror that tormented me almost constantly.

My life became hell. Do you remember that cleaning commercial with the neon-coloured bacteria on the person's hand? You would watch as the hand transferred the bacteria onto everything – door handles, surfaces, clothes ... *that's* how I saw the world: lit up like the Las Vegas strip, with neon bacteria covering every surface.

I had pretty much been contaminated as soon as I left the house in the morning. I would get to work, where, if I wanted to touch anywhere on my face, I had to first wash my hands. To make matters worse, I caught a cold at one point that winter, so blowing my runny nose every five minutes became a very tedious pain in the arse!

Washing my hands involved walking to the toilet, which meant opening three doors with my sleeve on the way. Once in the bathroom, I had to turn the tap on with my elbow (I got very good at doing things with my elbow, once the bruises from bashing it against the taps had faded), pump enough soap for five people into my hands, and rinse with scalding hot water.

This whole process – ensuring that I washed all the soap off properly (and repeating all the steps if I accidentally touched any part of the sink), then turning the tap off (again, with my elbow), and drying my hands with paper towels – probably took close to 10 minutes. Sometimes I would get caught in a loop of making tiny mistakes and having to start all over again. The all-too-familiar sick feeling of frustration returned, and I started to get tension headaches from concentrating so hard on everything I touched.

Eating was pretty much out of the question as, even with all my precautions, I didn't feel clean or safe enough touching food. Chocolate bars were just about all that was permissible, so long as I held them in the wrapper and didn't touch any part of the actual chocolate.

I worked 10-hour shifts during the busy Christmas period, sometimes running on just one chocolate bar. When I got home I'd be tearful, shaky, hungry, and dehydrated. It made me miserable to watch the guests around me laughing and enjoying their Christmas parties; they looked so carefree eating, drinking, and being merry. I remembered when Christmas used to be like that for me, and wondered how I'd reached a point where I was basically starving myself and washing my hands until they cracked and bled.

Even at home, my brain still didn't give me much respite. I had to shower and change as soon as I got home (what I jokingly – but not really – called my "decontamination process"), which was the last thing I felt like doing when I was practically running on empty.

Only then could I let myself eat and drink. From that point everything was plain sailing, right?

Of course it bloody wasn't.

I had to wash my hands in between every stage of preparing food. Even eating a packet of crisps was a four-step process.

1. Wash hands
2. Open crisps
3. Pour into bowl
4. Wash hands again

To my brain, that seemed like a reasonable precaution. Think of all the people with norovirus who could have touched that packet! It was lit up like the freakin' Blackpool Tower! Why was I the only person who could see this?

Basically, everything was a threat. Every surface was contaminated. I dreaded going to the crowded supermarket, full of potential germ carriers. *Which till do I use? Self-service? But I'd have to touch the screen. Regular till? But what if the cashier has been sick recently and touches all my stuff? If I pay by card I'll have to touch the PIN pad, but if I pay cash I'll have to handle dirty coins that have been touched by thousands of people …*

Dave knew what I was going through, but I don't think he quite realised the full extent of the thought and detail that went into all my precautionary steps. It was the same with the rest of my family and friends; to them it seemed like I still showed my usual "quirks", but they had no idea of the hell I was really going through. I found it such a hard thing to talk about because I wasn't in a place where I could be reasoned with. And I knew no one would really understand why I struggled so much in the first place – especially if I couldn't explain it myself.

I was always exhausted. Literally *everything* I did required planning and preparation. I envied the people around me who were going about their day, not thinking about *every little thing they were doing*. In the same way a mouse might constantly scan the skies for birds of prey, I was constantly scoping out the world around me, waiting for some unnamed predator to swoop down and sink its talons into me.

In winter, I always made sure to carry leather gloves with me, but I still had to make quick decisions about when I'd wear them and on which hand. If I knew I was going to be shaking someone's hand, I'd deliberately leave my gloves on. In the shop I'd wear one on my left hand to hold the basket. Couldn't have a glove touching the food, though, because that would contaminate it. I'm only realising now that this made no sense at all; to my eyes, everything was contaminated, so why should the glove matter?

This leads me on to one of the (many) other remarkably frustrating things I've learnt about mental illness: that there is no set rulebook to follow. The goalposts are constantly being moved and you're always frantically scrabbling to keep up with whatever it is your brain decides you should be doing. Just when you think you've figured everything out, you realise that even your own rules are made to be broken.

Sound ridiculous? Totally confusing? Frustrating as hell?

Yes, and it is. Because, once again, mental illness is an absolute son of a biscuit.

One of my safety behaviours was creating a mental ranking system of foods, places, and people who were safe. Only this is where the contradictions come into play.

Chicken: Dangerous, generally to be avoided. Acceptable only occasionally from certain reputable establishments. *No fast food under any circumstances.*

Pre-packed sandwiches / salads: Warning! Do not consume, unless from certain shops. It would seem that my emetophobia is frightfully middle-class, since for some reason "fancy" supermarkets like Sainsbury's, Waitrose or M&S were fine. I honestly don't know why; my only guess is that the "prestige" associated with the name, or the slightly higher price-tag, were indicators of trustworthiness.

Raw food, e.g. fruit: Fine if handled by me. If handled by others, do not eat.

Rice: Only fine if freshly cooked. *Never* reheated.

So, as you can see, each rule (and there were *many* more) had its own set of conditions and exceptions. It became easier to tell people that I didn't eat some of those things at all, rather than go into all my reasons. To this day, so many people think I don't like rice when actually I do – just not if it's been reheated.

And, of course, friends would see me eat chicken in one place, then question why I wouldn't let them cook it for me. It was never a reflection of how much I trusted them – in fact, one of the people on my "approved" list once gave himself food poisoning by undercooking chicken! Go figure. It goes to show that this stupid rule in my head was based on nothing.

Perhaps there were some inherent, subconscious factors at play, but there was nothing concrete that could stop my feelings of helplessness as I frantically trod water, trying to keep afloat in the sea of ridiculous, ever-changing rules thought up by my brain.

Let me tell you what else is hard about being an emetophobe in winter. As well as the daily struggle of going to work, feeding myself, and maintaining OTT levels of cleanliness, there was the constant dread of *so many social events*.

It is a constant challenge to stay vigilant when mingling with people you don't see very often, and in situations that quite often serve *finger food* (gulp ... my nightmare). *They have kids. What if their kids have been sick? So-and-so mentioned they weren't at work the other day. Did they have a bug?*

Listening for signs that someone has been ill, fighting the urge to interrogate them when they say they have been (let's be honest, no one likes to be asked exactly which orifice they've been leaking out of), and watching whose hands are touching what is kind of a party killer.

You have no choice but to put your trust in other people's food, homes, and cleanliness so much more over the festive season, and for a long time that trust didn't come easily to me.

I don't know how I got through that Christmas without keeling over or making myself ill. But in hindsight, even though I felt ill most of the time – headaches, anxiety, shakiness, etc. – I could have made myself a lot worse.

CHAPTER 5

2014

That winter was a nightmare, but afterwards things sort of went back to normal. This was always the way; my fears would come in crippling peaks and deceptive troughs. It became all too easy to kid myself I was fine during the summer months, when my anxiety pretty much all but eased off. I was still cautious with food, but there was no niggling fear of the dreaded norovirus to contend with.

By the time 2014 rolled around, I was still an event co-ordinator, but for a different company. More excitingly, after a long engagement, this was the year I would finally marry Dave.

But OCD, I learnt, doesn't care about ruining special occasions. In fact, it seems to relish it.

Two days before my wedding, I went to the beach with Dave and our best friends. We had a great time drinking cocktails and playing on a huge bouncy castle on the beach – this was a ridiculous idea in hindsight, as I almost gave myself a black eye right before my wedding day! Before we were about to leave, though, I washed my hands in the public loos. A bit of water from the sink splashed up at my mouth and I became convinced I was going to get a stomach bug right before the big day. What followed was a lot of tearful reassurance seeking, aimed at my best friend who has a medical background. She was so kind and patient, as she could see what a panic I'd managed to whip myself up into. I was so scared my wedding was about to be ruined! Visions of a re-enactment of the scene from *Bridesmaids* – where Maya Rudolph's character has to squat in the middle of the road in her wedding dress – danced in my head.

The next day, of course, I was fine. My friend was so sweet and told me how proud she was of how I'd coped with everything. Her praise made me swell with pride and happiness, even though I personally thought I'd handled it pretty badly.

I can look back now and see how ridiculous I was being in these situations. I try to remind myself of that whenever I start to worry about something. I tell myself that I've had these moments of panic in the past and nothing bad ever happened, so this will just be another instance of that. In a week or so I'll be able to look back on this moment and laugh about how I blew it out of proportion. This sort of thinking gives me some much-needed perspective and really helps me overcome bouts of anxiety.

The day itself was wonderful.

We had our ceremony at a local hotel. It was a quirky place with bright pink walls, golden pineapples hanging everywhere, and a suit of armour in the foyer. It was close enough to the beach that I knew we could get some amazing photos, and it was the sort of fun place that we felt suited us as a couple.

By this time, my relationship with my parents was probably as good as it would ever be. My mum didn't come to the wedding – her health meant she couldn't travel – but my dad was there to walk me down the aisle. I wasn't at all surprised, and in many ways I was relieved she wouldn't be there. I'd feared that she might find some way to upset me, or that she'd chew someone's ear off about government conspiracies.

I made my entrance to 'Dream' by Priscilla Ahn, and it was one of the most surreal and wonderful moments of my life. That was probably the part I was most nervous about, and I'd worked out the timing perfectly so that I would walk in during the climactic part of the song. Unfortunately, however, I didn't take into account just how little time it takes to walk down the aisle, and there ended up being a huge gap between my two bridesmaids entering and my big entrance. It was a lovely, awkward moment, with the staff trying to usher me in (they clearly thought I was about to do a runner), and a few nervous giggles from our guests.

Dave's mum did a beautiful reading from *Captain Corelli's Mandolin.* Before she went back to her seat, she told us how much she loves us and that she thinks we're invincible. That was just one of many unplanned but beautifully heartfelt moments of the day.

Afterwards, our guests put on their special wedding kippot as Dave's dad led the Jewish blessings. Friends and family took it in turns to read out various passages and showered us with blessings. They passed around a cup of ceremonial red wine (which didn't make me nervous in my white dress at *all*). Afterwards, everyone said what a wonderful part of the day that was.

Dave's cousin drove us to our reception in a beautiful white VW camper van. There, we ate, drank, laughed, and danced. We stood in the sunshine, drinking Pimm's and listening to an amazing acoustic guitarist. The atmosphere was everything we'd hoped for – relaxed and joyful. One of the highlights of this part of the day was when (upon my request) the guitarist played a strangely beautiful cover of 'Gangsta's Paradise', which has been a long-time favourite of mine and my two best friends' (both bridesmaids).

The speeches were heartfelt but hilarious, and the evening reception was so much fun. Our first dance was to John Legend's 'All of Me'. I think this was probably a lot of people's first dance in 2014, but despite it being highly unoriginal, I still love it. When we listened to it together, the lyrics spoke to us and just felt *right*. That said, if I were to do it all over again, I'd probably ignore the people who said this was a weird choice and have 'Where Is My Mind?' by The Pixies. I always think of this as mine and Dave's song because it was one of the first songs we spoke about together. Plus I just really, really love it.

Our second song was 'I See You Baby' by Groove Armada, which I must say was a solid choice on my part. Our DJ had warned us that no one would get on the dancefloor so soon after the first dance, but as soon as that song started playing, the party began. We danced, laughed, put on all the fancy dress items I'd bought for the photo booth, and raved to Pendulum.

A punk cover of 'Hava Nagila' played as Dave and I were hoisted up on chairs for the traditional Jewish dance, which was probably one of the single most terrifying moments of my life. I clung desperately to side of the chair (and the back of someone's neck, I believe – sorry to whoever that was!) trying not to slide off and break my leg.

The last song of the night was Feeder's 'Buck Rogers', which holds a very special place in my heart and was the perfect way to end the day on a high – it is optimistic, full of energy, and ideal for when people are all grabbing on to each other and doing a weird mix of drunken swaying and skanking.

Even though we no longer have a relationship, I will always cherish the special moments I shared with my dad throughout the day: how he was overcome with emotion as he told me I looked wonderful in my wedding dress; his amazing speech that got one of the biggest laughs of the day; the lovely, heartfelt words and stories he shared with us, and the fun we had putting on silly hats from the fancy dress box and dancing together.

As he is a stoic and fairly unemotional man, it was so special for me to see that side of him and watch him let his hair down and have some fun. I'd often felt sorry for him and the way he and my mother isolated themselves. They weren't close to their families and had no friends to speak of. I wondered how happy Dad was. Even now, I can't help but think about him. While logically I know he's a grown man, capable of making his own decisions, I often wonder if this is the life he'd have wanted for himself.

Perhaps that just helps me come to terms with what they later did to me. Maybe my mind doesn't want to let me believe that my sweet, kind father would turn against me in quite the spectacularly hurtful way he did.

Not too long after our wedding (and an incredible honeymoon at Lake Maggiore), I had a career change and became self-employed, taking over my father's work when he retired. I'd been looking for a change and his offer came at just the right time. It would be both the worst and best decision I could have made.

Hospitality had taken its toll on me; I was always either stressed, exhausted, or ill. I caught bug after bug and spent a week coming out in angry red hives – and all for a job that had become disheartening and thankless. I did, however, like organising events, and adored the client-facing nature of the job – perhaps an obvious sign that a career working from home wouldn't be right for me.

My dad worked in publishing, but not the exciting parts that most people think of. He worked in rights and permissions, which I reasoned I might not find thrilling, but it was at least a potential stepping stone to other opportunities within the industry. Little did I know that this decision would be the catalyst that brought my issues to an almighty head.

Initially, things were great. I didn't love the work, but the lifestyle suited me quite well. I liked being comfy at home, working in my PJs with Netflix on and basically living out everyone's dream of what working from home is like. I just about managed to stick to a schedule and stay relatively disciplined.

Then, as it likes to do, winter came around again. Unlike the previous years, I had no reason to leave the house now.

So I didn't.

I completely and utterly isolated myself. Why risk going to the shops when Dave could pop by on his way home?

Wait. How is Dave somehow impervious to stomach bugs?

That's a fair question, I suppose. We lived together, went to the same places, and ate the same things. So why was I confident that he wouldn't pick up any bugs, when he'd be going to the same shops and touching the same things as I would?

The answer once again, I'm afraid, is that mental illness is a completely illogical, irrational little knob that just likes to trick and deceive.

Not only did I irrationally fear certain people and places, but my OCD and emetophobia completely skewed the trust I had in myself too.

You'll be careless. You'll break the rules and touch something you shouldn't, a menacing voice would whisper in my ear.

I also reasoned that, since Dave was out anyway, he was already exposed to the dangers. I was safe in my bubble, so there was no sense exposing me as well.

That, or I guess I'm just lazy. But he knew this when he married me.

So I was isolated. Most days Dave was the only other person I'd speak to. I once went nine days without even leaving the house. When Dave came home, I'd be like an excited puppy waiting eagerly by the front door.

I wasn't good at working at home on my own. I missed having structure and colleagues to talk to. More than that, I think I just missed having a reason to put clothes on in the morning. I felt worthless and lonely and really, really bored. I needed to be stimulated creatively, but this job was just monotonous, repetitive data entry and admin. Every now and then there'd be a puzzle to solve, and I'd have to work really hard to track down a rights holder. I clung to those moments and told Dave all about them when he got home, with increasingly manic excitement.

Deep down, I'd known this about myself. I knew the job wouldn't be a good fit for me, but I'd wanted to make it work. My dad had been so excited that I was carrying on his work – he even mentioned how proud he was in his speech at my wedding. I felt like if I gave up I'd be letting him down.

I grew more and more miserable but I persevered. I became unreliable at work, missing deadlines and letting a lot of people down. I was trapped in this job by a misguided sense of familial obligation, but I felt unfulfilled.

I didn't tell Dad how I was feeling and, as we only really communicated by email, it was quite easy to hide how much I was drowning. I felt ashamed of myself but completely lacked the motivation to do anything about it.

Worse than that, I felt like a failure. I was lonely, unsuccessful, and hadn't achieved any of the things I thought I would have done by this point. I thought about teenage me, about to go to university and full of big dreams. What would she think about 27-year-old Mel, cooped up at home and earning no money doing a job she sucked at?

I can quite confidently say that she wouldn't have been too impressed.

I felt like all I was doing was lying to myself and everyone around me, desperately trying to act like everything was okay and that I didn't feel like my world was crumbling.

The world of online influencers quickly became my escape. I'd watch YouTubers and get sucked into their glamorous worlds. I didn't really know vlogging was a thing, but I liked how chatty the videos were; it was almost like hanging out with a friend. Then I learnt that blogging (that thing I did years ago, when I pretended to be super edgy on my LiveJournal account, then super emo on Myspace) was a real thing that people actually did as a job.

They still had their own little corners of the internet, but now they were beautiful, glossy places that looked like pages from a magazine. They shared their lives, what they ate, did and saw, and they were part of this great online community. They were the new trendsetters but also the relatable online "best friends".

I felt inspired. *I* could do this! Finally, I had something creative to channel some of my energy into again!

I closed my dusty, long-abandoned Twitter profile and set up a new one. I opened a WordPress account, bought a domain, and slowly tried to get the hang of Instagram.

In May 2015 my blog went live. I reinvented myself and began building my online brand.

I wasn't just Mel anymore. I was *Geek Magnifique*.

CHAPTER 6

COUNSELLING BEGINS

My new-found online life helped me immensely. There were always people I could talk to and when I couldn't cope with my life I'd just delve into someone else's. *Geek Magnifique* began as a place where I talked about wedding planning, film and TV, and anything else I was up to that I thought more than two other people might be interested in reading.

As anyone who's set up a blog knows, it won't bring you overnight success. It takes time to gain traction, especially on social media. Despite having since worked in marketing, I still think of it as a strange sort of witchcraft, and as much as you can analyse and use data to inform your strategy, there's still an element of luck. A post you think is absolutely genius may get no engagement, but a stupid tweet about a pigeon you saw flying along with a pack of crisps in his beak could get a thousand retweets. It's a trial and error process of getting to know your followers, finding your voice and what works for you. You have to put in the work to get yourself noticed.

I didn't really realise just how much you have to consider on the actual blog side of things too. I knew nothing about analytics, SEO, or Domain Authority. I'd sort of assumed it would be a "build it and they will come" type of situation.

I continued to fight the nagging feeling that I was going nowhere and would amount to nothing. I had my voice, sure, but it was getting lost. Approximately four people read my blog posts and I could see why; I wasn't doing anything new or different.

The worst part about being by myself all day, every day, was that it left me alone with my thoughts. With all that time to dwell, I'd find myself ruminating and taunting myself with every horrible thing that had or could happen to me.

After years of thinking I was absolutely fine, I was coming to realise that my childhood abuse had affected me more than I'd let myself believe. I knew I also had some issues to resolve with the rocky relationship I had with my parents too.

If I wasn't crying or panicking, I was lying on the sofa feeling completely and utterly flat. The anxiety would always be there, running in the background, but I felt too heavy, too physically exhausted to move. That was probably the worst feeling: the complete and total numbness. It was like my heart had slowed right down and I couldn't make myself feel anything. I was going nowhere. There was no point to anything. Something awful would probably happen to me anyway.

And so it went, round and round, in a horrible vicious cycle of fear, anxiety, apathy, sadness, and panic.

This crushing weight eventually became too much and, in a tearful moment of impulse, I left a voicemail for a Cognitive Behavioural Therapist I'd found online on the BABCP (British Association for Behavioural and Cognitive Psychotherapies) website.

I think I'd known for a while that I needed help. I can't even remember what happened in the moments before I made the phone call that pushed me to press that button and take the plunge.

Dave's father, Alfie, had been unwell for several months, and we'd recently found out that it was far more serious than we'd realised. Faced with the very real possibility of losing him, and the emotional toll that would take on the entire family, I think it became clear to me that I wasn't going to get through the coming months without some help.

I don't like saying I had depression, because I know how easily and often that term is thrown around. I was going through a difficult time, yes. Was I clinically depressed? Possibly, but also maybe not.

Was I suicidal? No. Sometimes I would cross the road without really looking and think to myself, *Oh well, if I get hit by a car, I get hit by a car.* Most days I wished I could stop existing, if only for a few hours.

What I wanted more than to end my own life was just to be able to press pause on everything around me. I wanted the time to rest and put myself back together with no interruptions. I wanted everything to stop completely and, when I was ready to re-join the world again, I wanted everything to be how I left it.

No one would be aware of my absence, and I wouldn't have people wondering why I wasn't replying to their texts – *that's* what I wanted. But sadly, things don't work like that. Turning your phone off only means you'll have more messages to reply to later.

It's such a helpless feeling, not wanting to exist but being too scared to die at the same time. You literally have no choice but to keep on going as things keep piling on top of you and each day gets a tiny bit harder.

So, I needed help. The therapist called me back and I was immediately reassured by her soft, comforting voice.

I'd chosen CBT after doing research about the best types of counselling for OCD and phobias. Once I'd weighed up the different options, it seemed like CBT was the best one for me.

The thought of talking to someone was daunting, to say the least. I felt like I had so many problems that there would be no way of knowing where to start. I feared I'd break apart completely, that I was unfixable.

I walked into my first session with Louisa not really knowing what to expect. Her office was softly lit, with a lovely scented candle burning in the corner.

I sat in the chair, she asked me something (probably a generic conversation opener, but I can't remember) and I burst into tears. I just sat there crying, letting everything out, despite having barely spoken to this person before. I felt so at ease and safe in her presence; I guess this was a good sign that I'd found the right counsellor.

When the tears finally dried up and, embarrassed, I mumbled an apology, she kindly told me I had nothing to be sorry for and that it was clear I had a lot I needed to get off my chest.

She started by asking me some questions. They were extremely direct, quick-fire, and personal, which I wasn't expecting (I thought there'd be a bit of "easing" into things).

'Are you suicidal?'

'No.'

'Have you ever been sexually abused?'

'Yes.'

I'm making this sound scary, but it's important to mention here that it really isn't. While counselling is tough (I won't sugar-coat it, therapy is draining and there will be plenty of times you'll just want to give up), the crucial thing to remember is it's a safe space. You can be open with your counsellor. Tell them if there's something you're finding particularly hard and help them set the pace. I had a lot of input and control over my own sessions. She would ask me which areas I felt I wanted to focus on and what my priorities were in terms of overcoming certain issues.

Of course, there were plenty of times when she challenged me, called me on it if she thought I was deliberately avoiding something, but if I ever got overwhelmed she would teach me ways to soothe myself. Sessions can – and often will – force you to confront things that heighten your anxiety. But again, it's vital to remember that you're in a safe and controlled environment.

Her office was near the beach, so I would sometimes pull over on the way home to just sit and stare at the sea. Quite often I'd stop somewhere nice for a coffee to clear my head. It just helped to have something nice to look forward to afterwards.

It's important to mention here that I opted for private sessions, for no real reason other than I didn't want to be put on a waiting list. And I wanted to have a choice about who I saw. I also didn't want to have a limit on the number of sessions I could have – my counsellor explained to me that 12 is the average number of sessions, but I instinctively felt that this wouldn't be enough for me.

I recall tearfully telling her I had no idea where to start – there were so many things I wanted to work through with her.

I told her about my OCD and phobia of vomiting. I explained my unhappy work situation and my strained relationship with my parents. I said that I was scared I was going to lose my father-in-law, and that I was terrified of how I was going to cope over the coming months, especially with Dave – my rock – not being able to support me as he normally would.

I knew I had to address the abuse and its impact on me. In fact, the more I dwelled on it, the more I started to feel like I wouldn't be able to forgive myself if I didn't come forward about what he did to me.

It's hard to remember in great detail how those early sessions went; they passed in a watery blur of unloading everything onto my counsellor. I would get to each session feeling like I was going to burst with things I needed to tell her about. But she helped me sift through the mess and prioritise what I wanted to tackle. We created a plan together, but acknowledged that life was unpredictable and that, on some weeks, new things might come up that would end up being more pressing.

I had a lot I wanted to achieve, but I was starting to understand that reaching your goals doesn't always quite look how you think it will. Sometimes resolving a relationship means ending it, rather than fixing it.

I wasn't going to leave counselling completely "cured", but I would be better equipped to handle life's challenges.

It wasn't going to help me understand everything about myself, but rather help me to accept that some things just *are*.

Most importantly, it wasn't going to give me all the answers, but it was going to help me take charge, decide what I really wanted and empower me to reach for it.

CHAPTER 7

OPENING UP ONLINE

I can't really remember what inspired me to open up about my mental health on my blog.

I actually started a different blog before deciding to really give things a shot with *Geek Magnifique*. I wrote a couple of posts about my emetophobia under a pen name. My first post was about a pepperoni pizza I'd ordered from Domino's. It was the first time I'd been brave enough to eat meat on a pizza in what seemed like years, and it felt like a huge (delicious) triumph. The next day I even reheated some, which was basically a double victory.

Geek Magnifique was never really supposed to be about mental health, though. It wasn't anonymous, but I was cautious about how open I was about my identity. I never posted photos of myself on social media, so writing about something so personal was a bit of a leap.

One day, I felt inspired to write a letter to my counsellor. It was a cathartic exercise that helped me process all the strides I'd taken and lessons I'd learnt.

When I finished, I had a decision to make – would I keep the letter private, or hit publish and send that part of myself out into the world?

A LETTER TO MY COUNSELLOR

I came to you because I'd become scared of the world around me.
Working from home, I'd started to isolate myself, closing off from friends and family. I was crippled by OCD and an overwhelming fear of vomiting that had me going to new and increasingly extreme lengths to "protect myself".

Sometimes I would go a week at a time without leaving the house. I would wash myself compulsively because I never felt clean. I never felt at ease. Simple, everyday decisions reduced me to tears or led to a panic attack, and I had moments so low that I simply couldn't see how I'd ever be happy again.

My family was going through a difficult time, and I knew things would get much worse before they got better. For the first time in my life I was faced with a loss I didn't know how to prepare myself for. Things are still hard, but they are getting better each day.

Issues from my past were resurfacing, and my relationships with those close to me were suffering. I remember confessing to you that I was afraid I was "unfixable". I couldn't see a light at the end of the tunnel.

I used to be afraid of everything, and I hated how weak that made me feel.
Once spontaneous, adventurous, and full of energy, I was now a shell of my former self. Thanks to you I know now that I'm not weak. Thanks to you I'm starting to feel positive about my future again.

CBT trains you to approach things differently and become your own counsellor, but you've taught me so much more than that. I've learnt to value and look after myself, and make my needs known to others. You've given me a voice again.

You've made me braver than I ever thought possible, and given me the courage to tackle things I never thought I could. You've given me the insight to understand myself, question my thought processes, and challenge my own negative thoughts. I still have my problems, but you've equipped me with the tools to tackle them better myself. I'm a million miles away from the person I was eight months ago.

Before, I couldn't wait to see you because I desperately needed an outlet.

I needed to vent, I needed you to help me organise my muddled thoughts. I needed to cry freely, without judgement.

Now I can't wait to see you because I want to tell you about a fear I conquered, or a new personal milestone I've achieved. No matter how tiny, you are always proud of me.

I couldn't stop smiling during my last session, because I started to feel like the pieces of my life were finally coming together. What we have worked through together has brought me a sense of direction again. It's brought me closure, vindication. It's shown me how to feel joy again.

I've never been suicidal, but there have been times when I've wished I could simply stop existing, just for a little while. Because no matter how much I shut myself away, turned off my phone, or ignored others, there would always come a point where I'd have to face it all again. I switched wildly between shaking with nervous energy and feeling so drained I couldn't move. I didn't care about sleeping, eating, or looking after myself. Nothing excited me anymore; I felt numb. That was the worst part; in the moments I didn't feel overwhelmed by fear or sadness, I longed to feel something but couldn't.

But there was a moment when it was like you helped me flick a switch.

Suddenly I felt alive again. Suddenly I felt fired up. I had goals, things to look forward to. I left that session full of hope and on my way home stopped to look out at the sea. I felt an incredible sense of calm and clarity.

I don't quite know how you do it, but you help me make sense of things. Sometimes the answer might be so obvious I can't believe I didn't see it myself. You help me realise that my needs and feelings are valid. You give me the confidence to ask for what I want, and the strength to make things happen for myself.

There's so much more I want to say, but no words can adequately sum up just how much you mean to me, or the impact you've had on my life in such a short space of time. You've helped me in more ways than I can count.

You've helped me to be me again.

We've laughed together and cried together. It's my last session with you soon, and I find it hard to think about my life without you in it. It's going to be a difficult goodbye, but I finally feel ready for it.

I hope you feel proud of the work you do, because you're amazing at it. It takes a truly special person to show someone the level of kindness, understanding, and compassion that you've shown me. I will never stop being thankful for everything you've done for me.

I will miss you, but I will never forget what you've taught me, or all the incredible things you've helped me to achieve. From the bottom of my heart, I thank you.

I figured there would be other people like me out there – scared, sad, and hopeless – who might get the courage they needed to reach out and ask for help. Or at the very least, feel less alone. So I posted it. Without even realising, I'd just taken the first step of a long and incredible journey to where I am today. I got a few nice comments from my relatively small following, which spurred me on to keep going. I was hesitant to share my blog on my personal Facebook page, because I was still unsure of how much I wanted my online persona to overlap with my real life.

It wasn't long, though, before I learnt that I wasn't the only person talking about their mental health online. Soon my eyes were opened to a vast community of bloggers on Twitter who were bravely and candidly sharing their experiences. I started taking part in #TalkMH, the Twitter mental health chat founded by fellow blogger Hannah Rainey. During these weekly chats we would focus on a particular topic (one of mine, for example, was the portrayal of mental health on TV), share our thoughts, and support each other. I felt emboldened by this and took the plunge, sharing my blog on Facebook, with all my IRL family and friends. The response I got was amazing. They were so supportive, told me I was brave for opening up, and even started to reach out to me and open up about their own struggles.

I learnt that there was more to being an online mental health advocate than just talking about your own experiences. From talking to other people, I broadened my knowledge of mental illness far further than my own conditions. I spoke to people with trichotillomania, BPD, compulsive skin-picking disorders. I discovered how to write sensitively about mental illness, appropriate language to use (for example, not using terms like "committing suicide" as it suggests criminality), and how to use trigger warnings. Several mental health blogger meetups were organised, and it was incredible to be in a room with so many people who were in the same boat as me. It felt like a safe space. As I watched a fellow OCD sufferer awkwardly eating his food with cutlery while everyone else used their hands, I felt a swell of comfort. I recognised so much of myself in him and I immediately felt less alone. These were my people and I could completely be myself around them.

I also found myself shouldering a lot of responsibility, in that strangers look to me for guidance and advice when they're struggling. I've always made it clear that I'm in no way a mental health professional. I have no medical knowledge; I'm merely sharing my own recovery journey. I can share what's helped me and signpost people to others that are qualified to help, for example GPs or counsellors.

Once, I came under criticism for passing on a recommendation for a natural anti-anxiety remedy that I hadn't actually used myself. I clearly said that I'd never used it, but had it recommended to me by a friend, which naturally led to questions of why I hadn't used it myself. Did I not trust it? Should I really be recommending things I haven't used? I felt that I'd been transparent and told them that I was simply relaying advice I'd been given by someone I trusted. From then on, though, I've always been cautious.

It's so tough, and everything I do is borne out of a genuine desire to pass on useful information and ultimately help people, but it's a fine line between that and perhaps giving advice you aren't qualified to give.

So, I'll say it again here: if you're struggling with anything I've talked about in this book, please talk to your GP. They will be able to advise the best course of action, whether that be medication, counselling, or both. Everything that's worked for me may also work for you – but then again, it may not.

I've also had a couple of scary situations where people have reached out to me when they've been in really dark places and I've feared for their lives. In these situations, I realised, the primary objective is to make sure they're not a danger to themselves. In one difficult instance I had a very distressed person send me a DM on Twitter. Their message implied that they were having thoughts of suicide, and shared some disturbing imagery that suggested how they were planning on doing it. When I tried to talk to them they responded incoherently. I felt at this point, with this person's life possibly in danger, I had no choice but to call the police. I gave them the person's Twitter handle, which happened to be their full name, along with whatever details I could glean from their profile about roughly where they lived.

The next day, I was informed that the person was fine. I got a message from them saying they weren't angry I called the police and they understood why I did it. From that point on, though, I also had to look after myself. I told them to reach out to their parents, GP, or mental health professional if they continued to have suicidal thoughts, then I distanced myself. I recognised that I was not equipped – emotionally or in a professional sense – to help them.

I will say, though, that doing what I do has been incredibly rewarding. When I share my posts and get messages from old friends who are struggling with something similar, and I'm able to point them in the right direction, I truly feel like I'm helping people – even if it's simply giving them the encouragement to reach out for help. Sometimes, all a person needs to hear is that they're not alone and that help is out there.

I get emails from people thanking me for sharing my story and asking me questions. I love that I'm helping to start conversations about mental health by being so open online, and it's hopefully helping others to be more understanding, patient, and compassionate towards those who are struggling.

CHAPTER 8

COMING FORWARD

I knew two things when I started having counselling. I knew that my relationship with my parents would be a big issue I'd want to talk through, and I also knew that I wanted to find the courage to come forward and speak out against my abuser. These two things butted heads with each other in my mind, as the third thing I knew was that my parents would never be supportive of me taking legal action against him. Coming forward was never explored as an option when I was a teenager and, even though I was an adult now, I knew my mother would still very much have a "sweep it under the rug" mentality – based on what, I don't know. Put it down to instinct, I guess. Though she made very little sense to me, I still got her, in a strange sort of way.

I guess I had never really questioned my mother's decision, I just trusted that she was doing what was right for me. She said she didn't want to put me through the trauma of going through a lengthy court process and, in some ways, I'm grateful that I didn't have to go through it when I was younger, now that I know just how hard it is. Even now, I don't blame her at all, even if I sometimes wish that she'd given me a bit more say in how things were handled – or at least made me feel like the issue was open for discussion.

For so long I thought there had to be something wrong with me. I knew that what my abuser had done to me was wrong, but I couldn't quite make myself feel any pain or anger towards him. And whenever I did lash out, it felt forced and unnatural.

When I shared that part of myself with Dave, we explored my feelings in great depth. I told him that I felt like I had to be dead inside. I wasn't traumatised in any of the ways you hear about, so surely there had to be something wrong with me.

I'd later realise that this was absolutely untrue, for two reasons:

1. Everyone is different, and there is no right way to cope with trauma. I can't stress this enough.
2. My trauma *had* affected me in so many ways; it just took me a long time to make the connection between how I was and what had happened to me.

I'm certain that my parents thought they were doing the right thing and I don't blame them in any way. As far as they were concerned, they'd severed ties with him, put a stop to it, and the matter was resolved.

But I think I needed the opportunity to work through it. I needed to talk it through, in order to process and understand what happened. I needed guidance, but instead the very fact that it was almost swept under the rug reinforced my view that I was making a big deal out of nothing.

I had boyfriends in my teenage years, but found it very hard to be intimate with them in any way – I couldn't bring myself to kiss my first boyfriend, despite caring for him deeply. When I was 18 I dated a much older man, which was definitely not the healthiest of choices now that I think about it. I attempted sex many times before it worked for me – it was almost like my body wouldn't let it happen.

Perhaps the most crucial realisation I came to, though, was thanks to a simple series of questions from my counsellor.

'How old were you when the abuse started?' she asked me.

'Eight.'

'And how old were you when the compulsions started?'

'Eight.'

'And you felt compelled to clean yourself obsessively?'

'Yes.'

Somehow, I still didn't see what she was getting at.

'And how did he make you feel?'

'Dirty.'

Oh.

Shit.

That realisation hit me like a slap across the face. It seemed so obvious as soon as she said it, but I'd never made the link before. How?

You hear a lot about people with OCD carrying out their rituals to stop something bad happening to their loved ones. I felt no such responsibility. My counsellor suggested that it was perhaps a way for me to have a sense of control, at a time in my life when control was slipping through my fingertips.

Of course, who really knows why our brains do or think anything? It's so much harder to establish causation. It's not like a physical injury – when you cut your finger with a knife, it bleeds. It's clear to see that one has caused the other. But I've come to realise that it's so much more complicated with mental health. Our minds are a mystery and we process things and cope with traumas in so many different, and often unpredictable, ways.

But this explanation felt so almost ridiculously textbook that it *had* to be right. It felt right.

There's an odd sort of comfort in understanding why you are the way you are. Even if the reason is just an educated guess, it helps.

Would things have turned out differently had I been given the support I needed from my parents? Perhaps, but it's not worth speculating.

Very early on in my sessions, I brought up that I wanted to finally speak up no matter what. I felt, deep down, that now was the time. I knew that this was the only way to finally close the door on that chapter of my life. I'd often worried that he could have gone on to do the same thing to other children, so I wanted to do it for that reason as well. I wanted to make sure that he couldn't carry on.

I remember my counsellor talking me through all the different options.

'We could ring the police together, now.'

My chest tightened. No, I wasn't ready for that.

'You could ring the police at home and we can talk it through in our next session.'

Better. Yes, I needed to do this alone, in private. But why was that so scary?

'I could ring them now, just to find out what will happen when you call them, if you'd like?'

Yes. I needed that. I needed some sort of idea of what to expect, and this at least didn't commit me to anything. I needed to know if I could turn back at any point, change my mind if I felt like I couldn't go any further.

My counsellor spoke to them for me and asked all the questions I had. Reassured that I could change my mind at any time, and that I'd never have to do anything I didn't want to do, I psyched myself up to make the call myself.

I did it one afternoon while I was home alone. I was shaking as I dialled the number, but I felt ready. A man answered the phone, which threw me slightly, but he had a warm and friendly voice so I felt reassured.

'I'd like to report the sexual abuse that happened to me as a child,' I stated, almost matter-of-factly.

Kindly, he asked me a few simple questions and took down some details, before explaining that someone would be in touch to book in an official interview. I wanted it over there and then, but looking back, I don't know how I thought it would be a case of going straight in and getting it done the same day.

I ended up being given an appointment with one of the detectives, for the following week, I think. It's sort of hard to remember the order everything happened in, or how long it all took. I don't know if that's a reflection of my mental state, or simply that the whole thing went on for so long that it's hard to keep track. I was somewhat relieved to learn that I would be speaking to a female officer – discussing what happened to me over the phone was one thing, but I didn't think I could handle talking to a man about it face-to-face.

CHAPTER 9

PANIC BUTTONS AND BRITNEY SPEARS

I think my police interview was at around four o'clock in the afternoon – or, at least, it was winter and I remember it was getting dark. I went down to the local police station and sat anxiously in the waiting area. There was a man at the counter who'd come in to pick up some of his belongings. For some reason he was told he wasn't allowed to, and he started to get quite agitated. I remember wishing they'd taken me somewhere away from all the noise, and I tried to distract myself on my phone. I hadn't told any of my close friends I was doing this; only Dave knew. He was very supportive, telling me all the time how strong he thought I was, and offering to be there for me in any way I needed.

The female officer who had been assigned to my case came through to greet me, and I was hit by a wave of relief. She looked warm and kind; maybe talking to her about this wouldn't be so bad.

She led me into the interview space, which was a strangely cold and sterile room dressed up to look like a cosy living room. Comfy sofas and cushions were set against cold, white walls. The video recording equipment in the corner and a box of tissues on the table reminded me that I wasn't just here for a nice chat and a cup of tea.

'Be careful not to touch that,' the officer told me, pointing to a black strip that ran along the wall. 'It's a panic button.' This served as another stark reminder of the unpleasantness of the situation.

We had a brief chat and she asked me a few questions. I guess she wanted to help me relax and ease into everything. She asked me what I did for a living and I told her I worked in publishing. She told me how well I'd done for myself and how it was amazing given what had happened to me. More often than not, she said, stories such as mine don't have happy endings.

My eyes welled up with tears. She seemed proud of me and I didn't deserve it. As far as I was concerned, I hadn't done well for myself at all.

Or maybe it was the way she was painting me as a victim that bothered me. I believe that only you can label yourself a victim, and that's never how I'd thought of myself.

It's funny, but I soon realised that there's no right word for this type of situation. No matter how nicely something is said, it can never sit quite right.

"Victim" feels too pitying, too sad.

"Witness" feels too inadequate. It detaches you from everything, like it didn't actually happen to you.

I heard both of these words a lot during the whole court process, and each time it was a reminder that the person speaking to me didn't really understand what I was going through. To them, it was a job. They probably spoke to hundreds of people just like me every year.

But to me, it was who I was. It was an experience I'd tried – and failed – to not let define me. If I had to pick a term, I'd probably choose "survivor". Rather than focusing on the sadness and struggles of past trauma, it highlights the strength of the people who've lived through it. Maybe it sounds cheesy, but I like it.

After our brief introductory chat, the camera started rolling. We began.

I told her I found it hard to just start talking about what happened, so she asked me some gentle, probing questions to start me off.

She encouraged me to be as detailed and factual as possible, but as I reeled off what had happened, I felt cold and robotic. If my case did go to court and a jury watched my evidence, what would they think of me? I probably came across as some sort of emotionless sociopath. It's awful recounting one of the worst experiences of your life, while mentally coaching yourself to be more likeable.

It felt wrong that I should be worrying about how I came across, but I couldn't stop myself.

I went through the events in as much of a logical order as I could, while she asked questions. I started to get frustrated; even though I knew she was doing her job, some of her questions seemed so irrelevant. Why was she picking up on tiny, insignificant details? Why did it matter which hand he touched me with? How on earth did she expect me to remember exactly what I was wearing, or how I was sitting?

I told her that it all started with inappropriate comments. He told me I "excited" him and referred to a time when I was running around naked in his flat "like I was asking for it". I couldn't have been more than five years old.

I told her about the time he took me to the beach and wordlessly slipped a hand down my top to squeeze my breast. The most ridiculous part of the whole thing was how embarrassed I was to tell the officer it was a Britney Spears CD he bought me afterwards. I said it was a CD, but I couldn't remember which one. I'd just described, in great detail, how a family friend had groped my breast, but I couldn't bring myself to admit liking Britney. It's strange, the things that go through your mind when you're being filmed in a strange room with a panic button.

We got to the morning of my 13th birthday and I could feel anxiety begin to rise inside me. My fingertips were cold and tingly and I could feel my chest tightening.

I heard myself reel off what happened and we discussed why he might have chosen that moment to do it. Then suddenly, a thought forced its way into my mind. I remembered his hands creeping lower, until they rested on my ...

'On your what?'

'My ... lower half.'

'Was this above or below your clothes?'

'Above.'

'So, what would you call that part of yourself?'

My mind was going through all the words for it, trying to settle on the most appropriate. Vagina.

'My—' I giggled nervously, feeling flushed and uncomfortable. 'My' – I gestured to the area in question – 'private region.'

'What word would you use? Don't be embarrassed, I've heard it all before.'

I couldn't do it. The word got stuck in my throat like a dry piece of bread. With a trembling voice, I asked to go to the bathroom.

Inside the stall – for some reason, the police toilets reminded me of school – I tried to calm myself. I remember there was a poster that made me laugh and I found myself wishing I had my phone to take a picture. Then I scolded myself for not being more serious. Everything felt so strange. I was in this completely alien and frightening situation, yet I could still find humour in something so silly. I told myself that I had no choice; I had to go back in there and just say what needed to be said. *Like ripping off a Band-aid.*

Back in the interview room, I did just that. I took a deep breath and, just like I did in my bedroom on the night of my 13th birthday, I bit the bullet. This was a new piece of information, the first time I'd said this out loud. I hadn't told my parents, my friends, Dave, or my counsellor, because I don't think I even remembered it had happened until about 15 minutes ago.

I felt like I was transported back to the night of my 13th birthday, sharing this huge secret for the very first time.

She picked things up where we'd left them. I took a deep breath.

'He put his hand on my vagina.'

As soon as that was said I felt weak with relief. I shook with adrenaline. Just as quickly, though, doubts started to creep in. Had I just lied? Why had I only just remembered that? What if it never happened? Maybe I'd panicked and felt like I needed to pad my story out.

I tried to shove down these irrational thoughts. No one prepares you for that. You worry that the police won't believe you, or your parents will think you're making it up. You never think that your mind will turn on you and start to doubt your story too.

'Look after yourself,' the officer told me kindly as I got ready to leave. 'Go home and eat some chocolate. Try not to drink any alcohol though.'

I nodded and smiled, all the while thinking about the bottle of wine I had waiting for me at home. Like hell I wasn't going to have a drink tonight.

CHAPTER 10

REBUILDING MYSELF

One of the most important things I've learnt is that there's no one right way to cope with the trauma of sexual abuse.

Throughout my teenage years, I didn't really think about what happened much. After the night I told my parents, it was mentioned maybe once more. Perhaps that lack of any sort of "aftermath" was why I didn't really feel anything. Maybe this was a good thing in some ways; the ties were severed and any talk of reporting it to the police was quickly dismissed – and that was that.

Without any sort of deeper analysis of how I felt (or a "debrief", as it were), it was almost easy to believe that what had happened was no big deal.

Over the years, I had many chats with Dave about how the abuse had affected me. Very often, I came to the conclusion that it hadn't.

'How is it possible that it didn't affect me?' I remember asking Dave one night in my university bedroom – and many times after that. Dave, understandably, was always at a loss for words. How do you even answer a question like that? He would just hold me, tell me that he didn't know the answer, but reassure me that he loved me no matter what.

You hear all the time about sexual abuse survivors and how they've been left traumatised. You read about the impact is has on them for years after, the inability to trust others, the PTSD, the never-ending nightmares.

How could I simply be *fine*? I knew I didn't possess some sort of exceptional emotional strength; in fact, I grew up constantly being told the opposite – that I was too sensitive.

The only thing I could think – that made any sense – was that I was somehow dead inside. Maybe I was so damaged that a little part of me, the part that feels pain or processes trauma, had just withered away. Of course, I learnt much later that this wasn't true.

I may not have been suffering from flashbacks or depression, but I was far from okay. My pain and confusion manifested itself in a constant state of fear. I was afraid of being sick, of being dirty; everything around me was a possible contaminant. I can see now that I viewed the world as an unsafe place – perhaps this was my brain's exaggerated response to what had happened, a way to keep me safe from any further trauma. But because my fear was so abstract, I didn't immediately link it to what happened.

For so long I viewed my fears, and my need to be clean, as personality quirks. It wasn't until they began to take over my life, and left me feeling like a shell of my former self, that I acknowledged they were more than that.

CHAPTER 11

EXPOSURE THERAPY

If you asked me to describe my perfect day, I'd probably have to say it would start with a lovely long lie-in followed by a tasty breakfast. Maybe coffee and pastries, or berries and yoghurt.

I'd get up and have a really nice hot shower before getting myself ready for the day.

Then I'd put my feet up and enjoy some nice relaxing videos of people vomiting.

After that, I'd probably have some lun—

Wait, what?

Sorry, did I make that bit too cheesy? I feel like it was the written equivalent of a record scratch. Hopefully though, it did actually make you do a bit of a double-take. Or, at the very least, question how much I've had to drink while writing this.

As much as we can agree on the fact that watching people "toss their cookies" (a gross expression that I've never really understood) is no one's idea of a good time, it's nevertheless what I found myself doing once a week for the best part of two or three months over the course of my counselling.

Even someone who has the smallest knowledge of counselling terminology will likely have heard of exposure therapy and have some idea of what it entails.

Afraid of spiders? Lock yourself in a room full of them. Terrified of clowns? Hire someone to dress as Pennywise and lurk menacingly in your back garden. It's basically facing your fears.

I'm obviously joking. Phobias are not to be taken lightly, and exposure therapy should be done in a safe and controlled environment by a professional. You dress up as a clown and hide in my back garden and you're getting yourself a punch in the balls. I think that's only fair.

While my main problem with emetophobia was the fear of physically being sick, I also had quite a severe aversion to seeing or hearing it, so my counsellor wanted to tackle this as well. We discussed in detail the various times I'd overheard people vomiting and how it made me feel. I told her that I had to block my ears or leave the room if someone was being sick on TV, or how I'd avoid certain movies if there was a good chance someone would vomit in them. I remember her asking me to describe exactly what it was about the sound of vomiting that I had an aversion to. I told her I didn't like the awful gurgling sound as the vomit rose up. To me, it sounded like the person was choking and gasping for air. I found the abrasive sound of retching too much to handle – it sounded painful and unnatural.

Exposure therapy sounds a bit scary, but there's really nothing to be afraid of. Firstly, you don't just dive straight in. And secondly, everything is safe, controlled, and at your own pace.

We started off small, to ease me in. I had to read lots of different words pertaining to vomit, say them out loud and, for the really challenging ones, write them myself. Remember when I mentioned superstitions? Well, that's where this all came to play for me.

If I even wrote the word "norovirus" down, I worried that the piece of paper would somehow become infectious and have the power to make me sick. I had to destroy it. If I ever Googled the word (and believe me, I did that a *lot* – remember "poogling"?), I had to delete my browser history for the same reason. Gives the concept of a computer virus a whole new meaning, doesn't it?

After I wrote the word down, slowly and calmly, I had to look at it on the page for a while. As I stared at it, willing myself to not break eye contact (that's how intimidating I found it – even in my retelling of this story I'm describing the word as if it were a person) and taking deep breaths, I had to focus on the anxiety I was feeling. My counsellor reminded me, as she always would when my anxiety flared up, that any physical sensations I was feeling weren't dangerous – they were merely a by-product of my nervous system misfiring.

Once I conquered this challenge, we moved on to pictures. At every step of the way she asked me if I was comfortable and we always took things at the pace I wanted.

We began with cartoon images of people vomiting; again, this was to ease me in and build my tolerance up slowly. Progress was slow and steady, over the course of a few weeks. Cartoons turned into photographs, followed by soundbites, then animated videos and, finally, real videos.

Before each one, she'd give me a brief description of what I was about to see, and we'd measure any anxiety the anticipation brought me. After I'd seen each one, she'd ask me how I found it. I started to notice that I felt more anxious before than after. The images were never as bad as I thought they were going to be. It started to strike me that perhaps a lot of my fear was rooted in the *anticipation* of being sick – the nausea and waiting for it to happen – rather than the actual event.

I remember one particular video was of a TV show host throwing up live on air. He handled it so calmly, even having a bit of a laugh afterwards. Other videos were also of people throwing up very publicly. My counsellor asked me how I'd feel if I was sick in front of loads of strangers. I said I'd find that horrible. She then asked me if the onlookers in the videos were super grossed out or horrified. When I thought about it, I realised they weren't.

I was starting to realise that a lot of my anxiety was rooted in the warped perceptions of vomiting that I'd created in my own head. I felt very strong emotions surrounding being sick – was it perhaps those imagined feelings of shame and unease that I was afraid of? I recalled times when I'd seen other children be sick in public. Afterwards, they'd looked ashamed and upset. The expressions on their faces would stay in my mind long afterwards and I felt strangely affected by that. Perhaps these experiences had stayed with me, and I feared feeling the way they had – shocked, embarrassed, and ashamed.

During my exposure therapy, I found watching other people just getting on with it and letting their bodies do what they needed weirdly reassuring. It was even more comforting to see that they were pretty much completely fine after it had happened. It was definitely a start, and I felt emboldened by this mini-breakthrough of sorts.

From then on, rather than scrunching my eyes shut and stuffing my fingers in my ears if I knew a scene with vomiting was coming up, I breathed through the anxiety and kept my eyes fixed on the screen.

At some point during all of this, Dave went out and had a few too many. When he came home and proceeded to be violently sick for several hours, rather than running away to the furthest point in the house, I sat outside the bathroom door to be with him. I even stayed in the room at one point. I didn't see him actually throwing up, but I heard it a lot, and made myself look in the toilet bowl after as well.

When I reported back to my counsellor, she was thrilled. 'I promise you I didn't orchestrate this somehow,' she laughed, but we both agreed that it was ideal timing and perfect exposure.

Of course, if Dave had been unwell with a stomach bug, I don't think I'd have been as brave. As much as I could handle seeing vomit, the risk of actually being sick myself still filled me with ice-cold dread.

But at this point, I was taking every little victory I could.

CHAPTER 12

MY OCD SUPERPOWERS

Before I start this chapter, I'd like to say, as a general disclaimer, that I'm in no way glamorising my mental illness, but rather poking fun at myself for all the ridiculous things it's made me do.

As a result of my OCD and emetophobia, I have become excellent at:

- **Assessing someone's physical health by analysing them in the manner of a criminal profiler.** I used to play a fun game in the supermarket called "Who's the least sickly-looking cashier?" One time I didn't trust my gut instinct, got chatting to the cashier, and she told me she'd been sick earlier that day. ACTUAL MAGICAL POWERS.

- **Changing a tyre with just my elbows.** Okay, so this one isn't strictly true, but you'd be amazed at the things I can do without my hands (insert Lorelai Gilmore exclamation of "dirty!" here). At one point I had bruises on my elbows from the amount of taps I turned, doors I opened, and things I picked up with them. I took the concept of "hands-free" to a whole new level.

- **Being impervious to scalding hot water** – if by "being impervious" you mean "being able to tolerate having permanently sore hands that were so red and dry they looked (and felt) like I was wearing gloves". Sexy.

- **My skin producing its own glutinous protective membrane, like a toad.** Fine, so that's another lie, but I did use so much alcohol gel that at times I was actually sticky to the touch. Did I already mention I'm sexy?

- **Overcooking food.** No one can transform a pizza into a tough, blackened Frisbee® quite like I can. Of course, I'll still seek reassurance that my food is cooked enough. Because yes, Mel – the peas you boiled for 10 minutes are going to somehow give you food poisoning.

- **Talking myself into believing that all of these things are perfectly sensible steps to avoiding harm.**

Although my OCD became predominantly contamination-based, sometimes the more ritualistic elements pop up again. The hardest thing for me to deal with on a fairly regular basis is needing conversations to go a particular way.

If I'm feeling especially anxious about something, or it's the first couple of days of my period, I start operating on high alert. If I feel like Dave isn't fully listening to me, or he responds slightly differently than I anticipate, I'll repeat what I said until I get the "right" outcome. There's no set number of times I feel like I have to do these things, I just keep going until the itch is scratched. If I'm feeling insecure, I won't seek reassurance just the once; I'll keep asking and asking, all the while actually making myself more and more anxious.

For a long time, Dave didn't know why I did these things and, of course, the more I'd repeat, the more frustrated he'd get. The more frustrated he got, the less likely he was to give me the answer I "needed" – and so the vicious cycle continued.

When I explored these issues in counselling, I found myself able to verbalise why I was doing these things, which helped Dave to understand and be better equipped to support me during times of anxiety. Rather than getting frustrated, he'll gently ask me why I'm repeating things. He'll ask me what's making me anxious, and we'll talk about it.

As you can probably imagine though, this still makes communicating difficult at times, and I often feel so frustrated at myself for not being able to have a normal conversation. When I'm really anxious, there's no such thing as making a comment in passing. Even if I say "thank you" and Dave doesn't say something back, I'll repeat until I get a "you're welcome". If I think back to primary school, I can remember that I would always repeat the word "sorry" to some of the other kids. I don't know why, or what I was apologising for, but I became known as the "girl who says sorry a lot". Some of the other kids found it funny, and it's not until recently that I've linked that behaviour to some of my other compulsions.

When I find myself getting stuck in a loop, I try to tell myself that I don't need to do these things. I think about how I'm making myself more anxious, and remind myself that I'm the only person standing in the way of feeling happy and relaxed. I use the word "joy" as a sort of mantra, to help me remember that I can choose my own happiness.

I know that this all comes from a deep-rooted fear of, and insecurity surrounding, not being listened to. As a kid, being ignored or interrupted would send me into fits of anger and distress.

If I think about it, that's probably been a constant thread running throughout my life. My relationship with my parents broke down largely because they refused to listen to my side of things. I never felt like they heard or respected me, or even tried to know me.

I've found that despite not being superstitious by nature, my OCD and emetophobia have given rise to some superstitious behaviour. For example, knocking on wood after saying the word "vomit", reluctance to say certain words for fear of "tempting fate", or an uncharacteristic or sudden belief in karma ('I can't do [insert "bad" thing here] or the universe will punish me by making me sick').

Added to my list of things my OCD makes me do that I'm ashamed of is spitting. If I accidentally touch my lips with "dirty" hands, or something splashes up towards my face, I feel like I have to spit to reduce the risk of getting sick from any contaminants. I hate spitting in public, but a few times I've felt compelled to. Cheers, OCD.

I think superstitions feed into OCD in a very natural way, and personally feel that if you know someone who's struggling, you shouldn't encourage superstitious behaviour. Even a light-hearted thought when someone makes an off-hand remark about the weather staying nice – such as *don't jinx it, knock on wood* – could encourage that sort of magical thinking, which in my experience can be quite damaging.

CHAPTER 13

MY FAVOURITE FATHER-IN-LAW

When I met Dave, I gained a second, wonderful family. They welcomed me into their home, supported me financially and emotionally, and introduced me to a cosy, warm version of family that I wasn't really used to.

It wasn't long after we got married that we were told that Dave's dad, Alfie, wasn't very well. Doctors had found a tumour and he was having treatment, but the details were kept vague and the word "chemotherapy" was never really used. For the most part, he carried on as normal and remained the relentlessly positive man he always was.

The following July he was in and out of hospital for various surgeries, but every time we went to visit him, he was still cheery and positive. Even now, I'm in awe of his strength and courage.

A bit later in the year, I saw a leaflet about palliative care in their kitchen. And though the situation was still being downplayed, it was getting harder and harder not to see the seriousness of his illness.

The day before Thanksgiving (Dave's mum is American, so we always have a lovely family meal), we all went to a hospital appointment with Alfie to speak to the specialist. This was the first time we all sat down with the doctor together.

We sat, in shock, as the consultant confirmed what we'd feared: they were no longer treating to cure him, but simply to keep him as comfortable as possible.

I then left the room with Alfie, to sit in the waiting area. While we chatted about our plans for the next few weeks, like nothing was going on, Dave asked how much longer he had left with his father. He was told three months.

It turned out to be just under two weeks.

We went back to the house after that awful hospital appointment and sat together feeling numb but tearful. Even Dave's mum, it would seem, hadn't fully grasped the severity of his illness – or was in denial, perhaps. We all tried to wrap our heads around the sudden and awful realisation that very soon we were going to lose him. All at once, we were going to lose a husband and a father, and, for me, a man who'd shown me generosity and kindness, who had welcomed me into his home and treated me like one of his own. After suspecting and fearing the worst for several weeks, in an odd way it was kind of a relief to have answers.

After Thanksgiving, Dave and I moved into his parents' house, to support where we could and spend as much time with Alfie as possible. In those dark and difficult weeks that followed, we learnt just how strong we were as a family. We banded together, supported each other, and did the best we could. None of us were really planning for what would happen after he passed. We were unable to fully get our heads around what life would be like, so we concentrated on getting by, one day at a time.

Then one day, we could tell something was very wrong. The doctor came around and told us that Alfie needed to go to hospital. There, we were told it was now a matter of days.

We had a running joke between us. Alfie called me his favourite daughter-in-law, and I called him my favourite father-in-law. That night in the hospital, knowing that it could well be the last, we all spent some time with him saying our goodbyes.

I told him I loved him, and he told me that I was more than just a daughter-in-law to him.

The next morning he passed, with all of us by his side. We'd known it was coming, but nothing can really prepare you, can it? Dave and his father were extremely close, and it hit him very hard.

The months that followed were some of the darkest I've experienced, as we muddled through and tried to figure out what to do next.

My counsellor would use tissues in a cup to demonstrate how our stressors and emotions can become too much. Each balled up tissue represented something that was causing pain or anxiety. Eventually, with too many tissues, that cup would overflow.

The first half of 2016 was a continuously overflowing cup. We were all grieving and struggling in our own ways. I had the stress and uncertainty of the court case hanging over me, knowing that it may very well drag out for a couple of years. I felt isolated and lost, with nothing to fulfil me. Then came the soul-destroying process of job hunting, and the steady breakdown of my relationship with my parents. It was a long, difficult period of despair, panic, loneliness, and emptiness, where at times it felt like nothing would bring us joy ever again.

It felt like everything was falling apart.

CHAPTER 14

HANDLE WITH CARE

I'd like to say my experience of the court system was a positive one, but it wasn't. It certainly wasn't horrendous, by any means, but there were ways I think I could have been treated better.

I was constantly reminded that my case was low priority. Of course, I appreciate that a historic case of sexual abuse is going to fall below crimes that are happening right now. But hearing things like, 'sorry things are taking so long, I've been really busy solving murders' isn't exactly comforting. Irrational as this may be, it felt like they were trivialising what had happened to me. Also, it rubbed me up the wrong way that it almost felt like he was bragging about catching murderers – did he expect me to fawn and say, 'Oh, well done!'?

As much as I didn't understand my parents' way of thinking, I got pretty good at predicting it. Unfortunately, I was not so good that they didn't manage to knock the wind out of me a couple of times, and ultimately, I wasn't good enough to make my way out of the minefield of our relationship unscathed. Dealing with my mother often felt like dealing with a volatile substance. Most of the time, I knew how to handle her without causing myself too much damage. But there were times – maybe I got too confident, too complacent – when I'd make one mistake, and send us both up in flames.

I was under no illusion that they'd support my decision to go to the police, which is why I put off telling them for as long as possible.

When it became clear that the police were going to want a statement from them, I knew I had no choice. With my best friend by my side, I bit the bullet and made the call. Keeping my voice as even and calm as I could, I told my mum that I had decided to go to the police about what happened to me all those years ago.

There was a beat of silence and then, 'Oh, Melissa. What have you done?'

My heart sank, and I felt tears prick behind my eyelids. I told her that I needed to do this, for closure.

'Closure,' she told me, 'comes from forgiveness.'

She didn't understand, just like I knew she wouldn't. I explained that it wasn't just about my own feelings, but about all the other people he could be harming. Firmly, and with surprising assertiveness, I told her I'd made my choice and that I knew I *had* to do this.

Unbelievably, she then tried to change the subject. 'So, what else have you been up to?'

My friend, who'd been holding my hand the whole time, looked at me with incredulity. 'Hang up!' she mouthed furiously at me.

I told my mother that I had to go, then sat in my friend's bedroom, as a strange feeling of intense anxiety and grief took over me, coupled with physical exhaustion. As I perched by the open French door, I struggled to take full breaths in. I cried, not hysterically, but wearily. I could almost feel my brain start to shut down, as I forced myself to stop thinking about her words and what this meant for the rest of the case. I didn't even realise in that moment that this conversation would spark the beginning of the end of my relationship with my parents.

After that day, emails were exchanged as my parents tried to chip away at my recollection of what happened. Looking back,

I should have visited them, or at least called, but I didn't feel like I was strong enough to argue with them. I didn't want to be worn down and I didn't want anyone changing my mind.

The police went to visit my parents and, predictably, they refused to sign a statement corroborating my retelling of events. I was sad, but not in the least bit surprised. I was hurt and annoyed, but I can't say I really felt betrayed. At least, not yet.

The timing of the whole case in general was terrible as well. I'd given my initial statement in November, just a few weeks before Alfie passed away. The rest of Dave's family had no idea what was going on; I wasn't ready to tell them about everything, and even if I had been, they had enough to deal with as it was. Though I knew in my heart I was doing the right thing, doubt began to chip away at me, and I questioned why I was putting myself through all this.

On one of the worst days I had a phone call with the detective, then had to pull myself together straightaway to attend a memorial service. The officer wanted to speak to Dave as well, and wasn't very sympathetic at all when I explained that now wasn't a good time. He ended up calling him anyway, and afterwards Dave was very upset by the lack of tact and sensitivity the detective had shown him. I was so angry and considered asking for a different detective to be assigned to the case. I decided that ultimately it probably wouldn't be worth the potential delays it could cause. I'd just grin and bear it and it would be over sooner, I told myself.

The whole ordeal ended up being worth it, as eventually I got a call telling me that they'd interviewed my abuser and he'd confessed to everything. We'd done it.

I started laughing, this weird sort of shaky laugh. The detective sounded genuinely pleased as he told me, 'See, even without your parents' support, you got justice. You got your redemption.'

I laughed some more at that, because "redemption" definitely seemed like the wrong word to use. It took me a little while of searching for the right one, before realising he meant "vindication".

I thought that was it. I felt like I'd locked a big, heavy door, turning the key with a loud, significant click. I could move on, after all these years.

I was wrong.

CHAPTER 15

THE LETTER

Things with my parents were tense for several months, until I told them that my abuser had confessed to everything, even without their statement. I also gathered the courage to tell them that I didn't want to work in publishing anymore. The response I got back was oddly supportive and kind. They said they were still fuzzy on what had happened, but they were glad I got the justice I needed. They were sad that I no longer wanted to carry on in my job, but they wanted me to be happy. I thought that was that. Finally, I'd be able to draw a line under this whole mess and start moving on.

Soon, Father's Day rolled around. Feeling much more positive about my relationship with my parents, I sent my dad a card. I thought absolutely nothing of it – why would I? It was simply a nice gesture.

A few weeks passed and I came home to find a letter addressed to me. I recognised my dad's handwriting and, despite the fact that he sent me mail fairly regularly, my blood ran cold. I knew – I just *knew* – this wasn't going to be good. Dave was right next to me as I stared at the envelope, and gave me a reassuring arm squeeze as I shakily told him who it was from.

I opened it with shaking hands and my eyes were immediately drawn to the opening words.

'You've no idea how deep the hurt is. It just keeps coming ...'

I was right. My gut instincts were right. Frantically, my eyes scanned the pages and it wasn't hard to grasp the gist.

I read the words over and over, feeling nothing. I was completely numb; I don't think the words sunk in right away.

When they did, a weight on my chest knocked the wind out of me. I was shaking as I handed the letter to Dave so he could read it.

The letter demanded a formal apology for sending my dad a Father's Day card when I hadn't sent Mum one, which had hurt them. Dad also questioned how strong my case was against my abuser, saying that he and Mum "had no idea what supposedly happened anyway" and so they felt unable to "rubber–stamp it" when the police asked for a statement. Why hadn't I discussed it with them before involving the police, so that they weren't caught off guard and so that it all made more sense to them? The police officer had – unbeknownst to me – turned up on their anniversary, and it had deeply upset them.

He told me that they'd had a visit from my abuser's partner, who trusted him implicitly with her grandchildren. Apparently, they'd "stabbed [my abuser] so deep in the heart" by shutting them out of their lives. Surely the police must have intimidated my abuser – an elderly, "vulnerable, probably senile" man, who had no proper funds or legal aid for defence?

Dad told me that Mum, who had "studied psychology since her twenties", suspected that I'd had a breakdown as a child. But what was particularly hurtful was that he questioned how emotionally damaged I'd been by the sexual abuse, claiming that "sexually damaged girls are very suspicious of the opposite sex". How old was I when I was hanging out with my first boyfriend, my second boyfriend, my 30-year-old boyfriend? How could that make sense for a sexually abused girl?

And then there was the closer: they loved me, but we needed to resolve everything in person and get it all out in the open face-to-face, as that was the only way that we could fix things.

Otherwise, I needn't bother.

It was awful.

Unable to process my thoughts clearly, I started doing a weird mixture of crying and laughing. My fingertips went numb and my chest tightened.

Dave read the letter and tried to hug me, but I needed to be alone. I sat on the toilet sobbing and trying to catch my breath, while he sat outside offering encouraging words.

I barely slept that night. After hyperventilating and crying in the bathroom, I snuggled up to Dave feeling empty. The words ran through my mind as I frantically tried to grasp their meaning, while already knowing, deep down, that there was no good to be taken from them.

Dave and I went around in endless circles, not really achieving any comfort or clarity. I don't think I could even begin processing my feelings, or healing, I just needed to vent. It was frustrating and upsetting; I felt sick and exhausted, both physically and mentally.

I couldn't quite wrap my head around all the awful things they'd said in that heinous letter. Instantly, I knew replying to them wasn't an option.

And where would I even start? Which disgusting accusation or ridiculous claim would I address first?

If I had to write out a response now, it would probably go something like this:

Dear Mum and Dad,

I know I'm not blameless in this. Perhaps I should have told you I was planning to go to the police. If I'm being honest, however, I never even planned to get you involved. If I'd had my way, you'd never even have known any of this was happening.

You use such harsh, cold words when referring to me in your letter, yet such emotive ones when talking about my abuser. "Stabbed him in the heart" – you use that phrase more than once.

Then you talk about your own pain, how "devastated" you were, how my actions made you look like "trash parents", and how you were cruelly deprived of your "anniversary treat". How is it you don't see how hard all this must have been for me?

How far down your fucking list of priorities do I come? You're not only more concerned about your own feelings, but you actually seem sympathetic towards him, the man who sexually abused me!

Then you bolster his partner's credentials – she's "very intelligent" – as if to, what, discredit me further?

We all know it was more than just inappropriate talk, even though you seem to be forgetting the other things I told you about. And even if it was just inappropriate talk – I was a fucking child. That's not acceptable.

In one of your earlier, equally heinous emails, you appear to defend him by claiming I seemed a lot more mature than I was. I was eight fucking years old – are you honestly suggesting I seemed like an adult to him?

And let's talk about these supposed "signs" of sexual abuse that you say weren't there, shall we?

You, in your own words, have said that I had a nervous breakdown when I was a child. I suppose that just happens, does it? My OCD just manifested itself, because that's what happens to healthy, happy children, right?

I never blamed you for what happened. There was no way you could have known, and as soon as you did, you took appropriate action and kept me safe from him. Thank you for that.

Why then, do you now decide to hurt me like this?

I was "comfortable" around boys, you say?

Well, as you're such an expert in psychology, perhaps you can explain to me why it is that I was physically unable to kiss my first boyfriend. That any time he came close, I'd pull away. And as for my 30-year-old boyfriend – I was 18 at the time, but I suppose you're going to tell me that that was a healthy, normal choice for a teenager to make?

I think we both know I'm not brave enough to confront you face-to-face, so this is the end of the road for us. You've shown you have no compassion for me, and I finally respect myself enough to stop putting us in situations where you can continue to hurt me.

My life will continue, and I will carry on being surrounded by people who love and support me. But in a few years, after all the missed birthdays and milestones, will you regret the relationship you've lost? I'm confident that I can pick myself up, keep going, and drag myself to a place where I can thrive. But you – where will you be?

I'm sad for you, truly I am. But you know what? I'm finally doing what I probably should have done a long time ago, and letting you go. So goodbye to you and all the hurt you've caused me. I won't let you make me doubt myself, or what happened to me, any longer.

Mel

The following morning, I contacted my counsellor to book in a session for as soon as possible. And because that wasn't soon enough, and I couldn't see a way out of my crushing sadness, I booked an appointment with my GP for later that day.

I'd been considering medication for quite some time, but bravo to my parents for actually giving me the final push I needed. I guess I should thank them really; who knows when – or even if – I would have sought help from my doctor. After everything – the isolation and loneliness, the bereavement, reliving my childhood abuse – it was a simple letter from my parents that ended up being the straw that broke the camel's back.

I walked into my doctor's office, sat on the cold plastic chair, and burst into tears. He treated me with kindness and patience, never once rushing me, and always reassuring me that I had nothing to be embarrassed about.

Honestly, I can't really remember what I told him. I think I blubbered about how I was struggling and couldn't cope anymore. I had been so reluctant to start taking medication (not because I was ashamed, but because I was afraid of the side effects, and becoming dependent on them), but at that moment I saw no other way to pull myself out of this dark, dark hole.

I remember feeling like I was spiralling out of control, and that this time there would be no fixing me. I used to joke to friends that I wanted to "give up on life". A small part of me wasn't joking; I couldn't see any sort of light at the end of this tunnel. I was taken back to the low point I was at when I started counselling. How was it possible that this stupid letter could push me back 20 steps, to where I started?

I needed help. I was desperate.

I was prescribed the lowest dose of sertraline, which is an SSRI (Selective Serotonin Reuptake Inhibitor). But it wasn't those little pills that gave me hope on that bleak day – it was four simple words uttered by my GP.

'You *will* get better.'

The kindness and sincerity in his voice – and the absolute certainty with which he assured me that I would be okay one day – filled me with something I hadn't ever felt before: hope.

CHAPTER 16

SERTRALINE DREAMS

I started taking my tablets that day. The doctor had warned me that the first three days would be the worst and that I should make myself a duvet nest on the sofa and rest. He also advised me that a common side effect of the medication is an upset stomach. As an emetophobe, this was obviously a big concern, but I'd reached a point where not even the possibility of vomiting would put me off trying something that could make me feel better.

For the first couple of days I felt strange. It's really hard to describe, but my muscles felt heavy, my head was woolly, and I felt like I was seeing my surroundings in slow motion. All my senses were dulled and I just lolled about on the sofa feeling numb and not quite there.

A few days in, Dave and I were having dinner when I put some broccoli in my mouth and instantly knew I had to stop eating. I was hit by a wave of nausea, the kind you get when you've stuffed your face with junk food and your body is telling you it's uncomfortably full.

Except I wasn't full – I'd only eaten a few mouthfuls – and I quickly realised that I hadn't managed to stave off the sertraline nausea. Sweat prickled at the back of my neck, and I felt anxiety begin to build. Cold dread clamped around my insides. I barely ate in the couple of days that followed, and I hated how weak I felt.

Had I done the right thing? Taking medication was a huge step, and one that I knew I shouldn't rush into. Had I just been so desperate for any sort of relief from my pain that I hadn't thought this through? My GP had spent a good half an hour with me, talking through everything I could expect, and answering my many questions. Suddenly, though, I couldn't remember anything we'd discussed.

So, less than a week into my first foil strip of tablets, I found myself having a phone appointment with the doctor, asking him what would happen if I stopped now. You have to be careful when coming off antidepressants (it should always be done with guidance from your GP), and while I assumed that being on the lowest possible dose (actually, I was taking half tablets at this point, so less than the smallest dose) for less than a week meant I wouldn't have any problems, I didn't feel confident making the decision alone. I think the real issue was I wanted to know all my options.

He reassured me that I could stop taking the medication without any worry, and that I could start again at a later date. I decided to stop; now wasn't the right time. I needed to think things through, and I wanted to have another face-to-face appointment with my GP to talk about things when I was feeling calmer and less emotional.

For the next few weeks the idea of medication was shelved, and I somehow managed to talk myself out of it. I really don't know why I was so reluctant; I was never ashamed – I think I was more worried that I'd become a different person, or experience horrible side effects.

I had so many conversations about it with Dave as well as friends, before finally going back to my GP with a proper plan of what I wanted to discuss with him. I asked all the questions I needed to, and once more he was patient, explained everything, and put my mind at ease. When I apologised for being an incoherent mess the first time, he very kindly told me I'd been absolutely fine. I also saw in his notes that he'd described me as "a little upset", which I thought was wildly generous.

He put me on the waiting list for further CBT sessions through a service called Steps to Wellbeing. He felt that it would be good to have it as an option further down the line and I agreed. My first counsellor had helped me immensely with a lot of very difficult things that were going on at that time, but now I felt that it could be good to knuckle down and tackle my ongoing issues with someone new.

I'm so grateful to that GP for his kindness, positivity, and the matter-of-fact way in which he told me that things might be a little bit shit at first, but I would get better. He never once made me feel silly, or like I was wasting his time, despite going well over my allocated 10 minutes for each appointment. I will always look back on those appointments as a turning point of sorts.

Overwhelmed by how positive my experience of opening up to a doctor had been, and hopeful that my story might give someone the encouragement they needed to do the same, I wrote a blog post, sharing my tips for getting the most out of your appointment (it's worth noting that this is based on my experience in the UK).

How to talk to your doctor about mental health

Discussing your mental health with a doctor for the first time might seem daunting, but you really needn't worry. Here are a few of my personal tips for getting the most out of your appointment and looking after yourself at the same time.

1. Book a double appointment if you think you'll need more than 10 minutes. I actually didn't know you could do this, but luckily my doctor spent a good half an hour with me anyway!
2. Don't be ashamed to cry. The doctor won't think you're being silly, they won't judge you and they most definitely will have seen it all before! Remember that doctors should be caring people by nature, and will only want to help you.

3. Be honest. You don't need to sugar-coat how you're feeling when you speak to a doctor. It will help them make a better decision about your treatment if you give them all the facts.

4. Take notes in with you. It's very easy to get muddled up or forget to mention things, especially if you're feeling overwhelmed or upset. Making the notes with someone close to you (only if you feel comfortable) could be a good idea too, as they'll be able to help you organise your thoughts and offer an outside perspective. Aim to be as clear as possible about how you feel, how long you've been feeling it for, and the impact it's having on your day-to-day life. For example, is it stopping you leaving the house, or affecting how well you take care of yourself?

5. Make sure you leave the appointment having understood your treatment plan. If you're prescribed medication, ask the doctor when they'll want to see you again to check in. They'll likely want to see you fairly regularly (at least at first) to make sure the medication and dosage is right for you. Have an idea of time frames and maybe even book your next appointment there and then (if possible).

6. Ask all the questions you need. Don't feel bad for doing this. You're not being a pain, that's what the doctor is there for, and they will ultimately want to reassure you. It's useful to have an idea of how long they expect you'll be on the medication for, and to know about any potential side effects. Ask if there's anything you should avoid – alcohol, other medications, natural supplements, etc.

7. Your usual doctor might not be the right one for you in this particular situation, but that's okay. If you don't feel listened to, supported or understood, don't be deterred. Your feelings are valid, so please don't start to doubt that. Instead seek out the care you deserve by making an appointment with a different doctor. It's important to have a GP you trust and feel comfortable with, as you'll likely see them quite regularly, at least at first.

8. You may well be asked some very direct and possibly uncomfortable questions. They'll likely ask if you've ever felt suicidal, or if you think you could be at risk of harming yourself. It might not be a pleasant conversation, but it's important to remember that these are routine questions and that the doctor is asking them with your best interests at heart. They're not there to judge you. Take your time answering, and please remember that there's never a wrong answer when it comes to how you're feeling. Whatever you say will simply help the doctor decide on the best treatment for you.

9. Remember, your doctor may be able to do more than just prescribe you medication. In the UK, GPs are able to refer you to local mental health services for counselling, and can even give advice on diet and lifestyle changes that may help. It's definitely worth a discussion with them, to explore your options. They may well ask you more general questions about your life (family, work, friends, etc.) to get a clearer picture of any other challenges you may be facing, as well as what kind of support system you have.

10. Be kind to yourself. Keep some time free after your appointment to do something that will make you happy. Maybe treat yourself to a hot chocolate, watch your favourite TV show, or have a nice long bath.

11. Lastly, and most importantly, never feel ashamed for seeking help. I can't stress this enough. *In no way does needing help make you weak, worthless or a burden.*

It takes a great deal of strength and courage to open up to another person, so be proud of yourself.

You are amazing and you *will* get through this.

Exactly as the doctor said, about three weeks into taking my tablets I started to feel different. I started to feel better.

The best way I can explain how sertraline helps me is this: it puts a cap on how much anxiety I can feel. If I start to feel myself spiralling, or get caught in a loop of compulsions, it's like my medication just ... cuts it off, like a blanket being thrown over a fire before it gets out of control.

It gives me a sort of clarity that helps me tune into my rational voice more, rather than listening to the illogical part of my brain as I would have done previously.

That's not to say that medication on its own would have been enough; I'm a firm believer that the lessons I learnt in CBT and the sertraline worked hand-in-hand. Therapy helped to change my mindset and put me in a much better place mentally; my medication did the rest.

Around that time, I spent a lovely evening with one of my best friends, talking and laughing like we used to. As we were saying goodbye, she pulled me into a tight hug and whispered in my ear, 'You feel like Mel again.' She was right; every day I could feel a little bit more of myself starting to come back and it was amazing to know that others could see it too.

I realised during this time that I'm a lot stronger than I give myself credit for, and that's something I hope everyone reading this will start to realise too.

When you're struggling with depression or anxiety, it's so easy to see yourself as weak or worthless. You're not. When the simplest of tasks feels like a steep, uphill climb, and every day feels like a battle, it takes a warrior to keep moving forward.

Please don't think for a second that admitting you're struggling is anything to be ashamed of either. The doctor told me that coming to him for help only proved how resilient I am. He made me feel strong at a time when I felt utterly broken, and I don't have the words to express how grateful I am for that.

I think it's important to give myself credit too. So, to myself I say:

Thank you for not giving up, even though you wanted to. Thank you for believing that happiness was out there and worth fighting for, with everything you had. Thank you for reaching out and seeking the help you knew you deserved. Thank you for realising that the right path isn't always the easiest, and thank you for having the courage to take it anyway.

It's so easy to thank the people around us who support us, but sometimes we need reminding that we're the ones who are putting in the hard graft.

Take some time to thank yourself, right now, and reflect on your achievements – no matter how small.

CHAPTER 17

SEVERING TIES

I knew with absolute certainty that my relationship with my parents was over, but I didn't know what to do about it. As much as part of me would have loved to actually send that letter I wrote, I knew no good could come of it.

I spoke to one of my friends, who told me I should simply mail their letter back to them with a note attached that made it clear, in no uncertain terms, that they were never to contact me again.

I was 90% sure that this was the right thing to do. It didn't leave anyone in limbo and, more importantly, it didn't leave me vulnerable to any further attacks.

I took the letter with me to my counselling session and gave it to my counsellor to read. I could see the odd look of surprise and confusion as she read the words out loud. I told her how I wanted to respond, and she encouraged me to explore all my other options.

My choices, as we both saw it, were to:

a. Do what my parents asked and either phone them, or visit them in person.

b. Arrange to have a group counselling session all together, in order to work through these issues, or

c. Sever contact.

I knew I wasn't strong enough to see them and I knew I couldn't deal with my mother face-to-face. I almost laughed at the suggestion of group counselling. There's no way I could arrange that. I would want it to be with my counsellor and there was just no feasible way we could orchestrate that. I was fairly confident my parents would not be open to that idea anyway, and I could just hear my mother asking why we would need some "quack" to come and fix our problems.

My counsellor helped me to detach myself from the emotions of the situation, in order to make a decision that was well reasoned and not impulsive. After a long and detailed discussion, we landed on my original plan. I'd explained to her that logistically, a group session wouldn't work, explored in great detail how unsafe I would feel seeing them in person, and ultimately that I felt I physically and emotionally wasn't capable of having any further interaction with them.

She told me that she wanted me to be able to look back and know I'd explored all my options, so that I wouldn't regret my decision. As I left her office, I knew I wouldn't. I'd made the right decision.

When I got home I got a Post-it note and wrote "NEVER contact me again", with "never" underlined twice (once didn't seem enough). I attached it to their letter, took it to the post office, and handed it to the person behind the counter.

'Is there anything valuable inside?' she asked me.

'No. Absolutely nothing,' I replied, knowing she was oblivious to the weight of my words.

I spent so long believing that my abuser hurt me worse than anyone ever could, and so I was completely blindsided when my parents managed to outdo him. Now that the court case is over, justice has been served, and I've got the closure I needed, the only real pain that remains comes from how they treated me. The dull ache of betrayal lingers at all times, like the embers of a fire. Every now and again, something stokes that fire and I feel its flames licking my insides.

It could be another birthday they miss, or simply the product of an ill-advised bout of rumination. I've chased myself round and around in circles, trying to find some logic in their actions. It's frustrating, pointless, and utterly miserable going over the same events in my head.

It's conflicting as well, because on the one hand I'm grateful that they respected my wishes to never contact me again, but on the other, I'm hurt that they didn't fight for me. It seems unfair that the burden was on me to go to them and make amends. Or that, somehow, they've made me the bad guy in this whole situation.

It's always been me that has had to go the extra mile and make all the apologies whenever there's been mutual wrongdoing.

'You're the parents!' I just want to scream at them, and remind them that whatever they might be feeling, it's their duty to be the bigger person. I can't understand how they could treat me with such little compassion. Did they honestly think so little of me that they believed I'd try to send an innocent man to jail? What for? To satisfy my boredom?

Even now, I still have nightmares where I'm shouting at them, begging them to listen as they yell over me and continue to attack me. In the dreams, I'm so anxious. I feel unheard and worthless. Sometimes I have dreams that I'm back in my home town and see my parents in a shop. I try to hide from them (and do an absolutely rubbish job, like a proper feet-poking-out-beneath-the-curtains type affair), but inevitably they see me. It's always the same look of confused horror on their face as they say my name. Sometimes Dream Mel talks to them, other times she runs away in that frustrating slow-motion way that only happens in dreams (or occasionally after a really big meal).

I wake up and wonder how they feel. Do they have regrets? Do they ever have dreams about me, about all the things they wish they could say to me? Do they feel any sort of remorse? I suspect not.

I'd love to believe that they've realised their mistake, or even that they have the tiniest idea of how much they've hurt me. I doubt it though.

There are a few odd things that still bring me a sort of wistful, lingering sadness.

I miss our family cat, who I very imaginatively named Funnycat. I feel so sad when I think about how I'll never see him again. He was big and soppy, and loved to cuddle me and lick my arms.

I have some things that belong to my parents – my dad's watch, an old photo and my mum's wedding ring – that I don't know what to do with. I fear that, if I send them back, I'll be opening up a dialogue again, which I don't want to do. I don't want it to be misinterpreted as some sort of deliberately hurtful act. I briefly considered selling them and donating the money to the local Rape Crisis team, or a similar service that helps people who've been victims of sexual assault. That didn't feel right either. So right now, the items are in an envelope in the glove compartment of my car, until I pluck up the courage to do something with them.

Before I lost touch with my parents, I found a really nice bottle of Schnapps in M&S that I thought Mum would really like. I never gave it to her, and I still see it on the shelf sometimes and feel sad. It's these silly, small things, that give me the odd tiny little stab of sadness when I least expect it.

Meeting new people and being asked about my family is tough, and answering questions from extended family about how my parents are doing can be tricky. I just try to be as vague as possible. I don't know why I don't quite feel like I can be honest with them. Sadly, I guess a small part of me worries that somehow, I'll come off looking like the bad guy. Whenever I actually do tell someone I don't have a relationship with my parents, I feel a little twinge of shame, like they'll think badly of me and assume I'm the horrible one. That probably says a lot about me, doesn't it?

I know there will probably be occasions in the future where I will attend a family function with my father there. The thought makes me come over all wheezy, but I'll cross that bridge when I come to it, I guess. I have this silly little delusion that if I could somehow talk to him, I could find the words to undo all the damage. In reality, I have no words. I would probably just stand there trying to force enough air into my lungs to stop myself from passing out.

I suspect that this hurt will continue to creep up on me every now and again, but I'm confident that, over time, it will start to happen less and less, until it's just an occasional whispering reminder.

CHAPTER 18

SAYING GOODBYE TO MY COUNSELLOR

I knew that saying goodbye to Louisa was going to be hard; indeed, for many sessions I couldn't even talk about when and how it would happen without getting really emotional. For months, I would go to her and spill my deepest, darkest fears, let out all my emotions, and depend on her for strength and perspective. It's such a unique and powerful relationship.

Over time, however, I realised that during all those sessions, she'd equipped me with the tools I needed to soothe myself. I became my own source of strength and clarity.

I still looked forward to seeing her, though, and I knew I'd miss her calming voice and welcoming office. I wanted my last session with her to be perfect, and she was great at working with me to make it exactly what I needed.

When the day arrived, I wore make-up rather than going barefaced as usual. I wore a nice dress and listened to feel-good music on the way. I felt emotional, but in a positive way. I guess the best word to describe it would be bittersweet.

I told her I would really like it if she recapped what we'd done together, so that it felt like we were reminiscing.

'We've been on quite a journey together,' she told me.

We also chatted about my new job and all the things I was looking forward to. I gave her a card, with a heartfelt message conveying the immense gratitude I felt. She'd warned me at the start that her eyes "might start leaking" at some point and as she read the card, they did. It was emotional and lovely and it still warms me to think about it.

At the end of the session she told me that I was courageous and that she believed I would often be in her thoughts. I was under no illusion that we had any sort of relationship other than a professional one, but I believed (and still do) that she truly did care about me.

I'll admit though, I still really miss her, even now.

CHAPTER 19

PULLING A SHAWSHANK

It was a difficult decision to leave publishing, but Louisa had helped me to see that I shouldn't stay in a job that made me unhappy. I remember after one of my sessions, I drove by the beach, as I often liked to do. It was a lovely day, and I had my music up loud. That Avicii song came on, the one about living a life you will remember, and I just felt this incredible rush of joy and hope. I was taking charge and doing something just for me, and it felt good. I had a goal and a sense of direction again. I wanted to find a creative role that put my love of writing and social media to good use. I felt positive about the future.

Trying to get myself back out into the world of work again was a lot harder than I thought it would be. Job hunting was tough. The first interview I had went so badly I was shaking in my seat. At one point I could feel a lump forming in my throat and had to try very hard to stop myself from bursting into tears. Needless to say, it was a no from them.

I had several other interviews and came so close on so many occasions. I started to feel like I did when I'd finished university – lost, hopeless, and like I would never get a job I loved.

Then I found Carrie, the owner of a local recruitment agency, who specialises in placing digital marketers. I met with her at a Starbucks and we ran through some interview-style questions.

Her questions weren't difficult, by any means, but for some reason they kept tripping me up. I felt like I had nothing to show for myself, and she quickly realised that my problem was my almost non-existent self-confidence.

She told me I was selling myself short, and picked bits out of my CV that I should feel proud of. We looked through a job spec she thought I might be suitable for, and whenever I said I didn't have experience in a particular area, she would find something on my CV that proved this wasn't the case.

I have a tendency to put myself down and highlight all the areas I'm lacking in. It might sound obvious, but when she told me to focus on my strengths instead, it was like a revelation.

She had a reassuring faith in me, and made me feel like finding a job was going to be a walk in the park.

Very soon after that meeting, I had an interview with an exciting new start-up company. Unlike the other interviews before it, I felt at ease and confident. I paced myself, focused on my strengths, and for some reason made up an absolute lie about spending all my spare time on the beach. Bizarre attempts to make myself sound more interesting aside, it felt like it went well.

I had a second interview, and within a few hours I got a call from Carrie telling me they wanted to make me an offer. I was in the middle of the card section of Asda and I remember hanging up the phone in a joyful daze. I'd done it. I'd got myself a job in marketing. Someone had taken a chance on me and I'd bagged myself my perfect job as a social media executive.

Getting back out into the world and working a regular nine-to-five in an office with actual people was a daunting prospect, but I knew with 100% certainty that I was doing the right thing.

Starting a new job and getting back out into the world again felt to me like pulling a Shawshank. Over the course of several months of job hunting, I'd slowly but surely tunnelled my way out of the sad little prison I'd built for myself. But, just like in

The Shawshank Redemption, I found life on the outside kind of difficult. My prison was also my comfort zone, my safety blanket, a little bubble in which I could do things at my own pace.

When I worked in events I was confident and personable. I conducted meetings with clients, led team briefings and travelled to other hotels around the country for training courses. At the time, none of these things felt like they were out of my comfort zone. Of course, I'd struggled with the workload and client demands at times, but I felt like I knew my job, and I was good at it. I went the extra mile, especially for brides, staying late to make sure I knew exactly how they wanted things, taking meetings when it suited them, and even just hanging out with their bridal parties and having a bit of a gossip. I truly loved what I did, and I cared about each and every one of my couples.

I'd helped to stuff brides (and their miles of lace and taffeta) into their wedding cars, personally drove to the local brewery to pick up a groom's favourite ale, showed family members to their rooms, and done all I could to make them feel taken care of. Moments of doubt were rare, and I felt like I was in my element.

So to now be starting completely from scratch, doing something I'd never really done before, felt almost impossible. When people asked me if I'd worked in marketing before, my blog and being "pretty good at social media" didn't feel like they carried much weight.

The office was very colourful and vibrant, full of interesting people and an office dog. It was a work environment I'd never really experienced before, and to go from complete isolation to somewhere so technicolour was a bit like sensory overload.

My first day, with all the introductions and getting to know my new colleagues, was the most interaction with new people I'd had in a very long time. I came home feeling emotionally drained, overthinking every exchange I'd had throughout the day and worrying I'd done or said something weird.

There were already so many things I didn't understand and there were times throughout the day I felt like I was about to cry. What if I couldn't do this? I didn't have any sort of marketing qualifications (other than something about the "marketing mix" I learnt in A Level business studies) and my new boss was quickly going to realise that my only real experience was spending a lot of time on Twitter. Not exactly impressive, right?

As the weeks went on, I got into a bit more of a rhythm, but I was still shocked at how many mundane things – everyday stuff that I used to do without a second thought, like calling someone on the phone, or having team meetings – suddenly felt massive. Any time I was asked a question I wasn't quite sure how to answer, I felt a swell of panic in my chest. Every tiny setback or complication made me feel teary and anxious. With work leaving me so exhausted, I often wanted to hide myself away at the end of the day. Quiet time became essential, and Dave was really good at giving me the space to come home and do what I needed to do, to decompress.

I was so frustrated. This wasn't me. I used to be confident. I wasn't afraid of talking to people. Why was I a shell of my former self?

I'm so grateful for the manager I had (Hi, Sam!), because very early on I was quite open with him about where I was at, mentally. I opened up to him about the difficult few months I'd been having, with the breakdown of my relationship with my parents. I told him that I got overwhelmed and anxious easily, and that I didn't have much faith in myself.

He was so understanding and perceptive. He could tell if I was struggling, and would send me out for some fresh air or a coffee. He challenged me, gave me constructive feedback, and praised good work, which bolstered my confidence. At lunch, we chatted about all sorts, and I found myself telling him about my mental health in much the same casual way one might mention they had a headache or a sore throat.

Of course, this is exactly how it should be in all workplaces, but I appreciate that not everyone is as fortunate as I was.

I soon found that I was going to need Sam's support more than I'd anticipated, when everything I thought was behind me – phone calls from the police, the whole horrible court case – came rushing back to pull the rug from under me one last time.

CHAPTER 20

UNKNOWN NUMBER

Calls from unknown numbers have a whole new meaning when you're wrapped up in anything that involves the police or CPS.

Whereas before I'd have just ignored them, or shrugged them off as spam calls, I quickly came to learn that calls from the police, CPS or Witness Care always come from unknown or withheld numbers.

Even now, I still get a little jolt of fear when "Unknown Number" flashes up on my phone, and memories of sneaking off to have painful conversations away from listening ears come flooding back.

I got one of these phone calls at work one day. I was in a meeting when my phone started vibrating. I saw those two words and I instantly felt on edge. My leg jiggled nervously for the rest of the meeting, and all I could think about was finding out what that call was about.

It was the lovely lady from Witness Care calling to see how I was, and to let me know what to expect when I arrived at court.

Wait, what?!

I wasn't going to court, I told her. Since he was pleading guilty, they wouldn't need me to appear. It was going to be open and shut, I thought.

'Oh,' she said, 'maybe there's been an error in communication, but as far as I'm aware, you'll have to appear.'

'I don't understand. He pleaded guilty,' I repeated, feeling like someone had scooped my insides out with a melon baller.

'I think the best thing for you to do is speak to the detective on your case and find out exactly what's going on.'

Shaking, I hung up and called him. He casually informed me that, in a very strange turn of events, my abuser was changing his plea.

But he'd already admitted to everything – how could this be happening?

The detective told me he'd never encountered a situation like this before. He suspected that the reality of the situation had hit my abuser and he'd panicked. He offered no explanation as to why I hadn't been told any of this sooner. I was so angry that I was finding out like this. He seemed to have no idea just how much this new development was going to impact me.

So, it wasn't a mistake. I was indeed going to need to appear in court. I can't even begin to describe how that felt. My medication was really helping to level me out, and I'd finally started a job I was really enjoying. That horrible year of darkness and despair was over and I was so close to actually feeling good again. The old me was coming back, slowly.

And now I had this horrible thing looming over me for goodness knows how many months. I wanted to be focusing on my job and getting my life back on track, but now I was going to have uncertainty and anxiety lurking at the back of my mind once more.

I went back to my desk feeling shell-shocked and numb. After a few moments of me staring blankly at my screen trying not to cry, Sam leant over and mouthed, 'Go, take a minute' with a kind smile and slight nod towards the door. I could not have been more grateful in that moment, to have someone so understanding looking out for me. I simply nodded in response, not wanting to draw extra attention to myself, or give away that something was wrong to the other two people in the office.

I wandered down the road to get a hot chocolate from Costa (coffee shops became my go-to happy place when I was struggling) and called Dave on the way. He helped me to calm down as I struggled to catch my breath, and reassured me that we would tackle this together.

Now it was a waiting game. I wouldn't know the court date until nearer the time. In general, I had no idea what to expect. I was offered the chance to sit in on a court case, to see what it was like, but that wasn't really of any interest to me. I'd sat in on various court cases before, for university, so I already knew what to expect on that front. What I *really* wanted to do was speak to the barrister representing me and ask him questions specific to my case. What's known as a "special measures" meeting was set up, and I was to travel to the CPS office in Hove.

Now, another frustrating thing about this whole process was that, because the majority of the offences took place in my home town, the whole investigation was being looked after by Sussex Police. It seemed unfair to me that I was going to have to travel back and forth, adding on additional stress and expense. Frustratingly, the trial could take place at one of three Crown Courts, but I wouldn't find out which until a few days beforehand.

All of this uncertainty and added stress was taking its toll on me, and I went back to the doctor. My previous GP had sadly left the practice and I was weirdly and disproportionately upset when I heard the news. I cried uncontrollably for most of the day, so much so that friends were concerned I'd become unhealthily attached.

They weren't wrong, I suppose. I think it's because he was the one I'd opened up to initially and I'd told him so much. The sexual abuse, my parents, *everything*. I'd placed so much trust in him, and felt so reassured by him, that I couldn't imagine embarking on what I suspected would be a long journey of taking antidepressants without him.

Thankfully, the next doctor was also really nice, but not quite as comforting. Rather than leaving his office feeling reassured, I had all these niggling little doubts colouring the very edges of my mind.

When I explained to him that I was having problems with anxiety as a result of the court case being dragged out, he looked at me with concern in his eyes and asked, 'Do you *actually* think you'll be okay? Are you going to get through this?'

He asked it kindly, and it was a clever question because it got me to open up, but I couldn't stop hearing those words in my head. In that moment I desperately wanted some sort of reassurance that I was going to be alright. Instead he looked at me with the worry of someone who wasn't convinced that was true.

I told him there are days when I wish I didn't exist. He asked me if I'd ever act on those thoughts. It's funny; the first time I was asked if I felt suicidal I flinched. I was shocked by the question, taken aback by the bluntness of its delivery. Not this time though; this was just a bit of casual back and forth.

I couldn't help but wonder how I got to this point. When did sitting in a doctor's office chatting about suicide become an average Wednesday morning?

As a result of the stress, I was increasingly relying on my safety behaviours to soothe myself, so he upped my dose of sertraline. He also prescribed beta blockers for the anxiety. I wasn't too worried about taking them, because they were more of an "as and when I needed them" type thing. The doctor was so casual about them, telling me stories about people taking them to get through a big presentation at work. Having them in my back pocket was a nice safety net.

About prescribing the beta blockers, my doctor told me: 'I can't change your world, but I can help in small ways.'

I was all lined up to have a few sessions of high-intensity CBT, to completely focus on the OCD and phobia side of things.

Looking back on my time with Louisa, I can see that what I needed more than anything was emotional support. I knew difficult times were ahead and I needed someone to give me the tools to cope with them.

This time, it felt like the experience was going to be more clinical, more focused. With this completely different mindset, I felt really positive about seeing my new therapist. The whole thing felt more structured; I knew I would likely only get the standard 12 sessions and so I wouldn't have the time to veer off into other issues.

Going into my first session with Anna, I felt so much stronger knowing what to expect. I was better prepared for her to delve deep into my compulsions and push me out of my comfort zone in the way I wasn't able to manage first time around. I felt ready for it and determined to conquer this once and for all.

Her room felt more like a GP's office than a relaxing space, which I think helped. I liked her; she was friendly but businesslike. For some reason, though, I wasn't prepared for the initial questions, despite knowing they were coming.

She got to the "have you ever been abused" question and I suddenly got choked up.

Perhaps it was the way the question was phrased; it was vague, the type of abuse not specified.

'I – I think so, I – d-don't know,' I stammered weakly.

How was it possible that, after everything I'd already been through, after all the times I'd had this conversation with complete strangers, that I was stumbling over this again?

Eventually I managed to calm myself down enough to tell her what was going on. I explained about the court case, and that I recently found out I was going to have to appear in court. I told her that I was terrified. I also briefly touched on the breakdown of my relationship with my parents. I thought if I could at least give her some context, and a better understanding of what was giving me anxiety, she'd be in a better position to help me.

CHAPTER 21

2017

2017 was the year my blog started to really take off. As well as being offered the abso-freaking-lutely amazing opportunity to write this book, I began to gain more exposure online and feel like an actual, proper blogger. Plus, I was invited to eat a lot of free pizza, and if that's not living the dream, I don't know what is.

I got a slightly unusual birthday present that year too, in the form of the ultimate exposure therapy: I *vomited*.

At one point, vomiting was so unimaginably awful to me that I would break down at the mere thought of it happening. But then, the day after my birthday weekend, I had my very own digestive reckoning.

I'd started feeling a little iffy over the weekend, but put it down to overindulging and the start of a cold. Feeling drained on the Monday evening after work, we ordered a pizza. I only managed a few slices (which is not like me at all) but, again, I attributed my lack of appetite to being run-down. A couple of hours later, I told Dave that I was feeling really rough and wanted to lie down. I felt fine as long as I stayed completely still, but even the slight turning of my head made me feel a bit queasy. I thought it was the pizza sitting heavy on my stomach, so I went to use the loo, and it was then that the nausea became real and much more urgent.

The familiar, visceral waves of fear washed over me, and I called out to Dave to bring me a bowl. He kept reassuring me that I wasn't going to be sick, but I knew I was.

I took stock of the sensations I was feeling; as I focused on how the cool glass felt against my fingertips, I knew my stomach was moments away from clenching, and my oesophagus would constrict violently in order to force out its contents.

'It's happening,' I called out to Dave, closing my eyes. In that moment I realised that I felt acceptance, rather than dread. As I retched, I took comfort in the way my body took over, doing what it needed to do. I tried to breathe through as best as I could. Afterwards, I laughed shakily as relief washed over me. The nausea was gone and I immediately felt better.

The bowl of my stomach contents smelt awful, and I didn't relish the thought of having to dispose of it. Slowly and carefully, I tipped it down the toilet, still shaking slightly as the adrenaline wore off. Afterwards, I brushed my teeth and showered, then went to bed. As unpleasant as the clean-up had been, I think having the bowl really helped. I realised then that one of my anxieties was rooted in the idea of vomiting in the toilet. I feared the splashback, and didn't like the idea of my head being so close to the loo. It turned out that having a clean bowl to be sick into, while sitting comfortably, made all the difference.

This was such a triumph for me that after it happened I couldn't quite believe how fine I felt. I immediately wanted to text Louisa. Even though I was no longer seeing her, I knew she'd understand the significance of what had happened. I sent her the message, and when she quickly replied to say that she was really happy for me, I felt a glow of pride. (Hallmark, it might be time to make some "congrats on the vomiting" cards. I'm just saying – there's definitely a market there.)

Just like that, everything changed, and I realised how far I'd come. I handled the clean-up in a very businesslike fashion, and remained calm at the prospect of it happening again (which it did, the next morning). I think the fact that I stayed so calm the first time gave me the confidence to just get on with it. The second time felt so uneventful, in fact, that it was almost just like any other bodily function.

At work, things were going great. I loved my colleagues and the super cool, Google-like office. I'd settled in and actually looked forward to going in every morning.

My main focus in my sessions with Anna was my OCD, my emetophobia, and tackling my safety behaviours.

One of the big goals that I worked on with her was to not feel contaminated by the outside world. I wanted to be able to come home after work and not feel like I *had* to shower immediately.

She wanted me to step into the house and put my "contaminated" feet up on the sofa, or pay extra close attention to each step I took on the carpet, really rubbing my feet in.

As I often did with my first counsellor, I felt a bit disheartened when it seemed like I was hitting up against a wall. I'd listen to her suggestions and exercises to do at home, nodding along while knowing full well there was no way I would be doing them. CBT very much forces you out of your comfort zone, by encouraging you to do the things that make you feel anxious, so that you can confront those feelings head-on. By this point, I think I'd grown weary of it. I had to try so hard to do normal things that most people didn't give a second thought to. Most days it just felt simpler to carry on with my safety behaviours.

I wanted her to say some magic words and flip some sort of switch in my brain that made me think like everyone else.

That said, I think I got a lot out of my sessions and I still felt very proud when I left her office for the last time.

Our goodbye wasn't emotional at all, but right before I left, she said to me: *'You did this.* It's not easy, but *you* did this.'

I can't tell you how proud her words made me feel. All the trust in myself, that I'd lost over the years, was coming back.

Recovery is possible. I hope that I'm proof of that.

In May, life decided to throw me a curveball, when my boss took me into the meeting room and told me I wouldn't be carrying on with the company. He said that he liked me, and thought I was good at my job, but that I just hadn't managed to get our social media to where it should be. I listened numbly, trying to make sense of his words and not really believing them. I made an impassioned, tearful plea, unwilling to accept what he was telling me; it was so sudden, so unexpected. I felt like I'd been punched in the stomach. The following day passed in a blur of tears and feeling very, very sorry for myself. Two days after I was let go, I went back into the office for my final day. I packed up my desk then spent most of my time trying to hold back tears.

My colleagues were lovely; they got me a card, gave me loads of hugs, took me for a coffee at lunchtime and for drinks after work. I left knowing I'd made some great friends. I'd never experienced working somewhere I really loved before, and the pain of losing my job was honestly akin to a break-up. Removing myself as admin from our social media accounts felt like changing my relationship status back to single. I still get a little pang of sadness when I see posts of my old colleagues at the office. The few weeks afterwards were a truly shit time. I comfort ate a lot of crap food and sherbet Dip Dabs and put on a stunning amount of weight.

In some ways, I guess it was a blessing in disguise. The court date had been set for June and I was sort of grateful that I didn't have to worry about taking time off work and trying to carry on as normal with everything else going on.

It was around that time that a friend of mine posted that she had a kitten that needed a good home. We'd planned to wait until we were in a house, but when I went around to visit him and saw his cheeky little face, I was in love. A few days later, I was excitedly stocking up on kitten supplies, ready to bring home our sweet little Marty (or Martin, when he's being naughty, which is most of the time). He filled our hearts with love, our lives with joy and, on several occasions, our home with poo. It was hard to deal with the additional mess, noise, and unpredictability that having a pet can bring, but Marty was so worth it. As he got older, he started to remind me of Funnycat, both in looks and the odd mannerism.

CHAPTER 22

THE COURT CASE

I had to be at Hove Crown Court first thing in the morning of Monday 26th June. We were offered a hotel stay, but I wanted to come home – even though this could mean a lot of travelling. I didn't mind though; I didn't want to be away from Marty, or have to worry about arranging for someone to feed him. We set off early and embarked on the two-hour journey to Hove. I was nervous and jittery, and spent most of the journey gibbering nonsense to try to distract myself. In times of stress, I really struggle with my OCD, so I found myself repeating things a lot and seeking extra reassurance. The phrases I repeat can vary according to what's going on at the time or how I'm feeling, but in this case, it was positive affirmations such as, 'Everything is going to be fine' and 'I'm going to cope with this'. I kept saying the words, as if there was a magic number that would make them come true. Sometimes Dave's tone would seem slightly off, or he wouldn't agree with me as emphatically as I'd have liked, so I would try again. It was exhausting. While there were times in the past where Dave might have grown frustrated, on this day he was wonderful at soothing me and keeping me relatively calm.

Once we got to the courthouse we were put in a strange, artificially homely room, where we sat on faded sofas and tried to pass the time as best we could. It was at this point that we started to feel a bit forgotten. We were left to wait there, with the odd sporadic update from a member of staff who didn't seem to really know what was going on. At one point, Dave went to find the vending machine and one of the staff unlocked a door for him. They then wandered off, leaving him trapped in the corridor. My chest was tight and my stomach fluttery, but I hesitated to take a propranolol. I have no idea why; I'm pretty sure this day was exactly why my doctor had given them to me.

Then we were moved into a smaller room used for video links. There were just a couple of chairs, a screen, and a camera. Still we waited. Unable to sit still or calm my thoughts, I finally took a beta blocker.

At about half past 11, we were told we weren't going to be needed until tomorrow. I was so disappointed and frustrated, I almost cried. I'd prepared myself for this, taken a propranolol to keep calm, and had it set in my head that by the end of the day everything would be over. Instead, we were now faced with a long drive back home, only to repeat everything again tomorrow. The adrenaline I was running on quickly wore off and I felt flat and drained.

Determined to get something positive out of our trip, we found a nice restaurant to have lunch in, then headed home and spent the rest of the day snuggling on the sofa.

Tuesday, take two. Having had our practice run, we were a well-oiled machine. We stopped at the same petrol station, where Dave, remembering what I'd chosen for breakfast the previous day, bought me a bottle of water and a strawberry cereal bar.

Knowing exactly what to expect this time, we pulled into the courthouse, breezed through security, and made our way up to the waiting room. The member of staff on duty seemed a lot more helpful than those the day before. She stayed with us, got to know us a bit, and answered our questions.

I didn't think twice about taking a propranolol this time, which really helped, and getting regular updates about timings made the whole thing a lot less frustrating than just being left in a room with no information.

As it got later and later into the afternoon, though, I started to worry. The court usher came back and told us that, unfortunately, there was a slight chance they were going to run out of time, and we might have to come back again tomorrow. For the second time, I felt like I might cry out of frustration. Though I knew there must be a reason for everything going the way it was, it felt so unfair that I was getting put through this each day.

In the end there was just enough time, and I found myself being guided through the labyrinth of corridors, to the courtroom. I sat in my little box, shielded from my abuser and unable to see anyone but a few members of the jury.

It's hard to remember exactly what happened, as I think I just kicked into survival mode, but I vividly recall being asked what felt like a lot of really mundane and irrelevant questions by the defence barrister.

I kept reminding myself that it was his job to discredit me. The thought made my insides clench with terror.

As part of the evidence, he read out several letters I wrote to my abuser as a child. They were all friendly and loving, each one talking about how much I was looking forward to his next visit. My heart sank as I realised what he was trying to do. He was trying to establish that I enjoyed my abuser's company and showed no outward signs of fearing him.

It was so surreal hearing him read back the words that my eight-year-old self wrote. At one point, he couldn't quite make out my handwriting and as he stumbled over the word, my abuser piped up, to clarify that the word was "shares". Hearing his voice again, I shuddered. I wasn't expecting to hear him. I don't know what else he said, but I remember the judge telling him to be quiet. It felt like I had someone in my corner and I was thankful for that.

The barrister picked apart every last detail of every visit, asked me strange questions designed to make my memory look unreliable and finally, after I told him my version of events, hit me with this:

'I'm going to put forward that everything you've just said is complete nonsense.'

Shit. Up until that moment, the questions had felt routine, back and forth, and almost mundane. I guess that was the point – to make it so that his accusation would come out of leftfield and throw me off balance.

It very nearly worked, but I'm incredibly proud of what happened next.

I took a deep breath and managed to keep my composure, despite my anger and shock. Calmly and evenly, I told him that it was in fact what actually happened, and that I was telling the truth. Everything he threw at me I calmly swatted aside. Even now, I don't quite know how I managed to tap into this well of strength and composure, but by fuck am I proud of myself!

A lot more nit-picking followed, as he tried to find some sort of hole in my account of what happened.

We got to the part about my abuser grabbing my breast under my top and, to my complete disbelief, the defence appeared to concede that the touching had happened, while merely disputing the squeeze I'd described afterwards.

I sat there, mouth agape, listening to a well-educated man in a wig suggest that a grown man touching a child's breast was fine, just as long as he didn't – what, squeeze it?

Was this a joke? Was he actually shitting me?!

Luckily, the judge, who'd been giving me a few reassuring glances throughout, was having none of this bullshit. She asked him to clarify that they were indeed admitting that the touching happened.

'Yes,' the barrister replied, once again adding that there had been no squeezing.

A feeling of elation rushed through me. Had we just won this? A member of the jury caught my eye and gave me a small smile.

After that, it was the prosecution's turn. He asked simple questions to help clarify some of the details of my account.

And then – it was over. I think I was in there for quite a long time (at least according to Dave), but it went by so quickly for me. As I was led out of the courtroom, I couldn't believe that was it. The usher was saying something to me, but I answered mechanically, unable to focus on anything but the chants of *I did it, I did it, I did it* that were running through my head.

CHAPTER 23

THE VERDICT

When the verdict came back guilty on all counts, none of us were surprised.

I'm angry that he changed his plea and put me through all that for nothing, but actually I'm also sort of glad that he had to hear me in court, strong, unwavering, and confident. I feel immensely proud of myself.

A sentencing date was set, and I planned to drive up to be there. I wanted to be in the room when it happened, not anxiously watching my phone waiting to hear the judge's decision.

As it turned out, I ended up starting a new job that week, but managed to get the day off. I was going to be a copywriter for a dental marketing agency. After I'd been laid off, my confidence was knocked, but it didn't take me too long to get back on my feet. I went on a few interviews for different marketing roles and took on a couple of freelance jobs before I was offered this role just a couple of months later. With some experience under my belt, and in a much better place emotionally, I came across as confident in my interviews – my job-hunting experience was a million times better than it had been this time last year.

My new role would involve liaising closely with clients, to create new marketing materials and website copy for them.

I was nervous but excited about doing something more client-facing again, and knew that I could call upon some of my skills I gained working in hospitality. However, I woke up on my first day feeling awful, and proceeded to vomit spectacularly all over my bedroom. (I stayed perfectly calm, by the way!)

I knew it wasn't great to call in sick on my first day, but I felt like I had no choice. I was also fairly confident that none of my new work colleagues would appreciate me throwing up all over my desk. I could tell my new boss wasn't too happy, as there was a big induction day planned for me. It wasn't ideal, he said, but "these things happen".

So, to get off on a marginally less terrible foot with my new boss, I gave up my day off for the sentencing.

The phone call came at about three o'clock on the Friday afternoon. Surrounded by new people I'd barely spoken to all week, I could not have felt more alone. I was sitting at a temporary desk away from everyone until mine was ready, and when lunchtime rolled around no one invited me to join them. I was too shy to muscle in, so I just kept myself to myself. It was very different to the lively and sociable office I'd just come from, and I felt somewhat disheartened. It seemed cliquey and my gut told me I wouldn't fit in here.

My abuser was given a suspended prison sentence, which meant jail time, but not for a further two years. In the meantime, he would be out on parole. In all likelihood, if he stayed on the right side of the law, he wouldn't end up behind bars at all.

I should have felt angry or deflated, but I guess all I really felt was indifferent. He had been found guilty, and that was all that really mattered. His relationship with his family had likely suffered and he would be made to sign the sex offenders' register. I guess that was justice enough. My relationship with my parents was destroyed, months of my life were turned into a nightmare, and I'd been forced to sit in a courtroom while a horrible, slimy-looking man told me he thought I was a liar.

If my abuser's family no longer trusted him, if just one of them couldn't bring themselves to look him in the eye, he would feel a fraction of the pain I was feeling. And that felt like justice to me.

Though my experience of the court system was pretty rubbish at times – whether it was the lack of sensitivity of the detective, the shambolic experience of our first wasted day in court, or the miscommunication I felt was happening between the police and Witness Care Officer – overall it got me what I needed.

I can't speak highly enough of the detective who took my initial statement. She was kind, compassionate, and even followed up with me to find out what the verdict was.

After everything was finished, it was all so surreal. I was left still reeling from the fallout with my parents, having constant nightmares and periods of deep sadness over what had happened – but in the eyes of the justice system, I was just another case closed. I got a very formal letter thanking me for my help on the case and for being a witness (there we go again with that word). I felt the usual bubble of outrage as I read the words over and over. I was seething with anger; it was a mixture of the blasé tone ("thanks for doing the justice system a solid, cheers mate") and the suggestion that I was in any way not completely at the epicentre of this whole thing.

I'd lost my parents over this, struggled with my mental health, had counselling *and* medication to cope with the whole ordeal, and suddenly I was just a witness?

I didn't just witness these things; I *lived* them. The lust in his voice still rang in my ears, the ghost of his fingers still cupped my breast and danced across the planes of my body.

How dare someone suggest that I wasn't right there, painfully aware of how trapped I was in my own body, as he slowly reached his hand down my top? Or how I'd wished more than anything that I could somehow jump out of my own skin and be somewhere, *anywhere* but here, as he forced me to kiss him?

Logically, I knew it was probably the best word they could have used. As I've already mentioned, I find "victim" very jarring. I believe that language is a powerful thing, and that nobody has the right to label you a victim but yourself. "Survivor", while commonly used to refer to someone who has experienced sexual abuse, is obviously not the sort of flowery, empowering word the CPS would use. So there we have it. *Witness*.

As a letter, it was generic and emotionless. It showed no sign of any understanding of the huge emotional upheaval and personal sacrifice this long and difficult journey had cost me. It felt like a bit of a slap in the face.

The decision to finally come forward after all these years was not one I made lightly. I needed a great deal of support and reassurance, and I can confidently say that I would never have done it without guidance from my counsellor.

It was never about punishment for me, and the thought of an old man sitting in jail didn't bring me any satisfaction. I think of him as pathetic; someone to be pitied. Knowing that a seed of doubt has been planted in the minds of everyone he knows, and that people will think twice before letting him near their children, is enough for me. As far as I'm concerned, justice has been served. It's finally over.

CHAPTER 24

A GOOD COCK

As time went on, I didn't settle into my new job. I enjoyed aspects of the role (and was surprisingly good at writing about teeth all day), but as predicted, I just didn't click with the team.

I did get one thing out of the job though – a sweet furry little brother for Marty. One of my colleagues was giving away a kitten and we'd been toying with the idea of finding a friend for Marty. He was such a loving, playful, and affectionate kitten that it seemed wrong for him to be home alone in the day while we were at work. When we came home he was always so full of restless energy that we thought having someone to play with would be really good for him.

When we first brought Plum home, it was hard. They fought constantly and had to be kept separate for the first couple of weeks. We knew cats are very territorial and that Marty would take a little bit of time to adjust, but they were simply incapable of spending any time together without biting and hissing at each other.

I started to worry we'd made a mistake, but we followed the advice the vet gave us and introduced them to each other slowly. Eventually they got used to each other and now they are absolutely adorable together. They snuggle up together, look after and wash each other. When Plum was poorly, Marty sat under the bed and wrapped himself around his little brother. If either of them goes to the vet for any reason, when we return the other will run to the cat carrier and sniff through the bars to check they're alright.

It wasn't long before I found another job. Purely by chance, I stumbled on a job posting that seemed perfect for me. I applied for it that night, and was very quickly offered a first interview. I knew I'd feel like an absolute twat handing in my notice so soon, but I knew it made more sense to do it this way, rather than staying in a job I knew wasn't right for me. I'm very much a "gut instinct" type person, and the more I was told about the role, the more I wanted it.

Somewhat disappointingly, however, I felt like I'd fluffed the first interview. I'd floundered when asked to suggest a possible social media campaign and left feeling so frustrated I could have cried.

Determined to redeem myself, I worked on a pitch for the second interview. When they asked me how I felt the first one had gone, I told them I was disappointed that I didn't answer their question better, and if they'd let me, I'd like to run them through the strategy I'd put together. As I handed them my printouts and talked them through my ideas, I felt like I was back in my element. Afterwards, I got to spend some time with the people who would be my new colleagues. As I fell into relaxed, easy conversation with them, and we bounced ideas off each other, I knew I'd nailed it.

Despite a less than ideal start (I realised when I arrived that I'd put my shirt on back-to-front, and had to start my interview with a quick trip to the toilets to sort myself out!), by the time I walked back out those doors I was triumphant. I'd just given the interview of my life, and I knew they'd be making me an offer.

The role was very similar to my first social media job and when I found myself slipping back into my comfort zone, I knew I'd made the right choice. It doesn't take me long to unleash my weirdness in a new job, but this time I broke the ice a little quicker than expected.

In a group Skype chat, we were talking about a team night out and suggesting places to go. I soon discovered the worst place you can possibly hit the enter key by mistake:

"I love me a good cock—"

A moment of horrified silence passed, swiftly followed by everyone bursting out laughing at the same time.

"—tail" I finished typing feebly, as if there was somehow any saving the situation.

As mortifying as that moment was, it made me realise that these were my kind of people, and from then on, we built a strong friendship founded on mutual respect, a similar (filthy) sense of humour, and a healthy amount of mockery.

It's a special kind of magic when you find yourself part of a team that works really well together, and this is what we had. We bounced ideas off each other and made each other laugh and, for the second time in my career, I was lucky enough to experience the joy of feeling fired up creatively. Nothing is more satisfying than having that "lightbulb" moment and feeling your ideas click into place.

I was at work when I got the call to tell me that I officially had this book deal, and Team Awesome were the first people I told. Even though I've since moved on, I know that I've made some lasting friends.

CHAPTER 25

CHILDREN

You might be wondering how my emetophobia has affected my feelings about having children.

The truth is, I used to have serious doubts about having children, for two main reasons:

1. My phobias

Even though my emetophobia is much more manageable now, I can't pretend that the idea of a potential nine months of constant nausea and vomiting doesn't completely horrify me. The thought makes my blood go cold. Not just that, but the idea of being so much at the mercy of my body, unable to stop it from changing so dramatically, is not something I'm comfortable with at all.

But I said, "phobias", plural, didn't I?

Much like my OCD and emetophobia feed into each other, my emetophobia shares a very symbiotic relationship and many overlaps with another phobia: tokophobia. Tokophobia is the phobia of childbirth.

Without going into the full spiel about phobias all over again, I'm more than aware that probably all women are afraid to some extent of giving birth. It's said to be the worst pain a person can experience. Who wouldn't be afraid?

But my aversion goes so much deeper than that. If I see a woman giving birth on TV, or even just a stock photo of a woman pretending to be in labour, I feel an all-consuming terror and revulsion.

I used to try to watch *One Born Every Minute* (I guess out of morbid curiosity, or perhaps even as a form of exposure), but all I saw was the women's faces contorted in agony, bloated and grotesque, grunting like animals as they were ravaged by unbearable pain. It all seemed so primal to me, and I couldn't stand the thought of being at my body's mercy once labour starts.

I became obsessed with reading real-life birth stories, in the same way people enjoy reading horror novels – I didn't want to keep reading, but I couldn't tear my eyes away either.

Afterwards I would think, *there's absolutely no way I could go through that.*

2. I used to think I wouldn't be a good mother.

My parents put too much on my shoulders. Because I hadn't wanted to move away, my mother blamed me for "trapping them there forever" when house prices in our home town went up. It feels to me now like my parents were never really willing to factor me into their lifestyle and resented me for "holding them back". They certainly found many ways to make me aware of this fact.

It's taken me a long time to come around to believing that I'd actually make a good parent. When our best friends had their beautiful baby, Dylan, I fell in love with him. Since then, I've thoroughly loved being Aunty Mel, and getting to see him grow and blossom into this amazing little person. I love buying him presents, doing silly things to make his face break out into his adorable little gummy smile, and when he falls asleep on me, his chunky baby arms wrapped around me and his gentle snores tickling the nape of my neck, I feel like my heart could burst.

Seeing how much Dave loves spending time with him, blowing raspberries to make him laugh, cuddling him, and singing ridiculous songs to him has made me realise that parenthood will be a joyful time.

Obviously it will be hard, and of course I'm scared, but I'm excited to say that we're currently exploring our options for having a family. With more of our friends having children (and knowing that we have a loving support network in place), I feel like we won't be alone.

I think about our little family, and how the last couple of years have shown me just how strong and happy we are as a couple, and my heart swells with excitement at embarking on this adventure together.

CHAPTER 26

HOW TO SURVIVE BEING AWKWARD AF

I've spoken a lot about how I sometimes find conversations difficult, and can be overly sensitive or critical of myself. I've talked about how hard I found it to integrate back into the real world, and how social interactions often left me feeling drained and exhausted. But I've come out of the other side of this and learnt a lesson or two about how to cope with socialising when you'd feel more comfortable being a hermit halfway up a mountain somewhere.

Here are some of the things I tell myself:

It's okay to make mistakes.

Life isn't scripted. Sometimes we mess up our words or accidentally interrupt each other. That's absolutely fine. Again, make a little joke, or apologise if you've interrupted someone, but don't sweat it. We're all human.

It's not always up to you to fill the silence.

Obviously if you're hosting a dinner party, you probably should try to keep the conversation flowing. But I'm talking more about those awkward situations at work – you know the ones. Whether you're trying to make a cup of tea around someone washing up their Tupperware, or enduring a silent ride in the lift with your boss, it's important to remember that it's not your responsibility to fill the silence. Remind yourself that they're not saying anything either, so if they're happy being quiet, you can be too.

We're all in the same boat.

Worried the person you met at that party last weekend thinks it's really weird that you kissed them on both cheeks? Chances are, they're sitting at home stressing about the fact they shook your hand when you left, rather than giving you a hug. We can all do it from time to time. Many of us with social anxiety lie awake at night, replaying these moments in our heads. Chances are, they might be too busy worrying about how they came across, to think about anything you did.

We are all flapping and squawking our way awkwardly through life, so don't sweat it.

It's fine to step away from situations that make you anxious.

Sometimes I find large gatherings very overwhelming, especially with a lot of people I don't know. If things become too much I excuse myself to go to the loo, or step outside for a moment of fresh air. No one's going to think you're rude or weird, and it's okay to be honest with people. If someone judges you for telling them you need a moment to clear your head, then quite frankly there are probably better people you could be spending your time with!

Other things that can help:

Have a drink in your hand.

In social gatherings I often like to have a drink in my hand. And no, it's not because I'm a booze hound; the drink doesn't have to be alcohol. Having something to hold (that isn't my phone) means I don't gesticulate wildly, which I found made me feel very flustered when I talked. It also gives one of my hands something to do, as I often feel self-conscious about how I'm holding myself and what I'm doing with my hands. I find it really helpful to have something to sip while I talk, as it lets me pace myself, stops my mouth from getting dry, and gives me a couple of seconds to clear my head if I've lost my train of thought during a conversation.

Don't be afraid to laugh at yourself.

I've learnt to make jokes if I accidentally say something silly. I know – it's easier said than done, and it definitely takes time. But I've really found that by not taking myself too seriously and just embracing my own ridiculousness, I've become much more relaxed in social situations.

Say no.

I try not to plan too many social events in one week, as I know I need time to recharge. You don't have to accept every invitation – your friends will understand. Use whatever helps you feel organised, whether it's a paper diary or the calendar on your phone, to manage your social life. Not only will planning ahead help you feel more in control, but scheduling regular self-care time is a great way to avoid feeling burnt out. By being more selective, you'll find that the social events you do go to are so much more enjoyable.

Don't be embarrassed to ask for help.

Turning up to a large gathering by yourself can feel really daunting. If there's going to be someone there you know, why not ask them to come out and meet you at the door so you can walk in together? Obviously this won't always be an option, but when it is, please don't feel too embarrassed to ask. They're not going to think you're being silly but again, if for some reason they do, I would argue that there are plenty more supportive and understanding people you could be hanging out with.

Just be honest.

Everyone has certain things that make them uncomfortable. What makes your needs any less important than someone else's?

For example, if you don't feel safe in crowded places, let your loved ones know. In the same way they probably wouldn't take their vegetarian friend to a steak restaurant, they shouldn't want to take you somewhere that makes you feel anxious either. Your needs matter and you deserve to surround yourself with people who are considerate of your feelings.

CHAPTER 27

MENTAL HEALTH AND FAITH

Within the online mental health community, I've met quite a few people who draw strength from their faith in God. I myself have often spoken openly about how I don't have any such faith.

On a practical level, I believe I've found the right people to help me – my loved ones, my GP, and counsellors – but would additional spiritual guidance help me too? The truth is, I don't know.

In fact, my lack of faith is something that used to bother me. I explored the possibilities, asked questions, even prayed for a sign that God exists. As I got older, though, I accepted that my beliefs were what they were, and I was still a good person with plenty to offer.

Religion became quite important when I met Dave, as he and his family are Jewish and quite observant. Early on, I made it clear I wasn't going to convert, but I was happy enough to take part in Jewish holidays, learn how to say the Hebrew blessings, and incorporate Jewish customs into our wedding. They were mostly fine with me not converting, though it did come up every now and again.

There have been times when my lack of faith has caused tension and upset. At times, my openness has been met with shock and disappointment. I started to feel like some of the feelings of acceptance I'd been feeling were based on a false impression held of me, as a good Christian girl. I couldn't understand why anyone's feelings about me would change just because I didn't believe in God. I was still exactly the same person who treated those around me with love and compassion.

These feelings all came up in my counselling sessions, and I described how upset I was that I somehow felt like less of a person because of my lack of religious beliefs. Counselling helped me to feel more confident and assertive, and I began to realise that my views, though different, were still valid. I became more outspoken and didn't back down from discussion.

Previously, I'd feel so sad and deflated that I'd just give up and let the conversation fizzle out. Or I felt like there was no way to make the other person understand my point of view and I'd become overwhelmed. Afterwards I'd just feel angry. The people who love you are supposed to accept you, and I didn't feel accepted. This was a big part of me that they wanted to change, even going so far as to say that I was confused, or that I "couldn't possibly believe" what I did. In a way, their attitude and lack of willingness to try to understand my beliefs was reminiscent of how my own parents would try to bulldoze my opinions, and I experienced the similar feelings of frustration at not being heard.

But gradually I learnt that my feelings were just as important as everyone else's, and realised I was doing myself a disservice by not being honest about who I was. This issue has brought me a lot of anxiety over the years and I simply don't see why. Surely I should be judged on my actions and values, rather than my faith?

The point I'm trying to make is this: we are all different. Each of us is raised differently, with different values and beliefs. Regardless of faith, sexuality or any other factor, we are all worthy of love and compassion. All I've ever wanted is a sense of belonging, and I felt like my beliefs were standing in the way of this.

Within the context of mental illness recovery, I've heard people suggest prayer as a treatment option. Of course I understand how faith can be a huge source of comfort and guidance, but I think it's dangerous to suggest it in place of support from a medical professional. You wouldn't just pray for God to mend a broken leg, so why a broken mind? Please don't ever feel like your mental health isn't worthy of a doctor's time – it's just as valid as your physical health.

CHAPTER 28

I'VE COME A LONG WAY

Now to talk about some of my personal triumphs, because it's really important to remind ourselves (especially if we're ever feeling disheartened) of all the amazing strides we've taken, and all the milestones we've had – no matter how insignificant they may seem to others. Trigger warning: there is going to be a lot of poo and puke talk in this chapter. Please feel free to skip ahead if you feel more comfortable. I won't be offended, I promise.

I can handle poo now. Sort of.

The entrance to our flat was at the end of a pathway we affectionately nicknamed "Shit Alley", for fairly obvious reasons. That alleyway used to make me dread leaving or coming home. I would check my shoes compulsively to make sure I hadn't stepped in anything.

There's a technique used in filmmaking called a "dolly zoom", where the camera zooms in on something while simultaneously being moved backwards on a dolly. You know in a horror film, when the camera is looking down a creepy hallway and starts to move forward, except there's this weird effect that makes it look like the corridor is stretching out?

Well, I would leave my house in the morning, look down that alleyway and start to feel like I was in one of those long, creepy horror film corridors. What was, in reality, just a few metres felt like a mile.

The way I would shimmy along on my tiptoes, stretching and jumping over certain areas, always reminded me of a diamond thief navigating a grid of lasers.

Somewhere along the line though, my attitude towards poo changed, and I suspect it was partly down to the lovable little rapscallion we call Marty.

We quickly learnt three things about cats:

1. They might be known for being clean animals, but kittens weirdly aren't that bothered about being covered in their own poo. Not ideal.
2. Marty sure looks cute, but don't let him fool you – he can kick up a shitstorm like nobody else I've come across.
3. "Litter-trained" means *diddly squat*. Marty was renowned for dropping the odd surprise deuce at the bottom of the stairs. I very quickly became acquainted with Vanish carpet cleaner and the wonderful sensation of cupping a nice warm turd in my hand. It's sublime, in case you were wondering.

It was a steep learning curve that very often pushed me out of my comfort zone. But looking back, it might just have been the best exposure therapy I could have had. Or at the very least, the cutest.

Once I learnt and trusted that poo could be cleaned off carpets (plus bedsheets, toe beans and, at times, myself), suddenly the prospect of wiping a bit of poo off the sole of my shoe didn't seem like such a big deal.

A few years back, Dave stepped in the tiniest little blob of really old, dried-up poo. There was literally *nothing* at all on his shoes, and most people wouldn't have given it a second thought, but I had a complete hysterical panic attack. I was hyperventilating and crying and couldn't calm my racing thoughts. I spiralled so hard and so quickly that I frightened myself. I made Dave throw those shoes away and gave him detailed and specific instructions for how to clean the downstairs hallway. I sought constant reassurance afterwards that everything was clean and "decontaminated". He was amazing, of course. 'Don't worry,' he reassured me, 'I was going to replace those shoes soon anyway.' I'm sure he was puzzled by my overreaction, but he was kind and patient with me.

This was one of the things I really hated, when I was at my worst; not only was I living like this, but I was forcing Dave to do so as well.

Recently, however, in bright, technicolour contrast, Dave told me that he'd stepped in poo on the way home. He told me how he took his shoes off at the door, then went through to the back garden and cleaned them. I've always said that I want him to be honest with me about any poopy accidents, but I would have completely understood had he been nervous to tell me.

I was about to ask follow-up questions and fall back into my former pattern of reassurance seeking, but the rational side of me just said "no". Dave told me he'd taken care of it and I trusted that. When I asked Dave if he was surprised at how calmly I reacted, he simply shrugged and said, 'Not really. You're so much better now with all that stuff.' I beamed with pride.

That's all there was to it. I was amazed at how, in the space of just a couple of years, I'd come so far. I'd finally learnt to listen to my rational brain and could cope with situations like that without blowing them up into a huge, distressing ordeal. Being calmer and more logical was so freeing! This was one of those small but amazing moments in which I felt like a "normal" person again.

If you're in a similar boat to me and having pets seems like an insurmountable challenge from a contamination point of view, please don't let that put you off. It's tough at first, but so, so worth it.

All I can say with cats is prepare to hoover up a lot of litter, get a good carpet spray designed for pet messes, and, though fleas are inevitable (and complete bastards), by treating your pet (and your home) religiously and just persevering, you'll win the battle.

I've saved a ton on shoes.

No, I'm not about to reveal to you my dangerous addiction to Jimmy Choos – in reality, the truth is far less glamorous.

On my walk to work (which of course started with the aforementioned causeway of crap), I would check my shoes several times to make sure I hadn't trodden in something. If I spied even the smallest speck of anything remotely faecal-looking, I would abandon my shoes and put on the brand-new pair I carried with me at all times.

I felt awful doing this as I was literally stepping out of my shoes and leaving them on the pavement (I couldn't touch them, because then my hands would be "contaminated").

A few times, people would spot pairs of abandoned shoes in places I often went, and they would question me about it.

Once, a colleague of mine said that there was always a pair of black ballet pumps in the staff parking area. He said it looked like whoever was wearing them had been lifted straight out of them. He'd picked the shoes up, in case they were mine.

'How strange,' I tried to laugh breezily, before lying and telling him they weren't mine.

Jim, if you're reading this, you were right. I was just too embarrassed to tell you.

They were only £6 Asda black pumps, but I dread to think how many pairs I burnt through. If I were to try to add up how much I spent, I'm sure I'd be horrified. For this reason, I was always reluctant to buy myself nice shoes, and I felt pretty sad about that. Now though, I have a few lovely pairs of shoes, and while I'm still conscious of where I step and always check my shoes before going into the house, I have the much more logical mindset of "everything can be cleaned". If I were to tread in something, I know now that I would be able to deal with it, calmly. For example, I now smell any suspicious marks on my shoes, and trust my judgement. If it don't smell, it ain't shit. I occasionally have the odd lapse, but I'm able to enjoy wearing nice shoes again, safe in the knowledge that if an accident were to happen, I'd feel equipped to simply clean it up.

I was able to partake of the poultry.

Cooking chicken at home became a huge no-no for me, and I would only eat it in restaurants on very rare occasions. Though I often felt a bit nervous, I managed to get to a point where I'd let friends cook it for me, and even became partial to a cheeky Nando's. I've since become a vegetarian (for reasons unrelated to emetophobia), but I confidently reached a point where I was cooking and eating sausages, prawns, pre-packed sandwiches and loads of other foods I would have previously been too nervous to eat.

I now wash my hands less.

I still wash my hands more than the average bear, but nowhere near as much as before. My positive experiences with vomiting have put things into perspective for me. While I'm not completely over my emetophobia – the anxiety definitely still pops up from time to time – knowing that I've now vomited several times and handled it like a pro has made me much more relaxed about the whole business. When you're not quite so afraid of being sick, the "need" for safety behaviours – such as excessive handwashing – starts to diminish as well. The website, Emetophobia Help, was also a useful resource for me, especially for setting me straight when it came to fear of stomach bugs.

Understanding the ways in which bugs like norovirus can and can't be transmitted – and that some of my safety behaviours were actually a complete waste of time – really changed my whole outlook. I became much calmer, and I now find it so much easier to ignore irrational thoughts.

CHAPTER 29

BOW CHEDDAR WOW WOW

CBT was difficult for me – I won't sugar-coat that. The point of a lot of the exercises is to trigger anxiety, then address and challenge it. I learnt that I had to go against my safety behaviours, especially on difficult days when I longed to give in to them. A lot of the time, giving in and going for my seventh shower of the day felt like the easiest option. At least then I wouldn't have to try to cope with the feelings of dirtiness, the unease, and the intrusive thoughts. But I knew that this was just putting a bandage on the problem, rather than addressing the root cause – my irrational thoughts.

My way to avoid compulsive showering eventually became going to the bathroom as little as possible. I stopped drinking water, which meant I often suffered from headaches, fatigue, and dry, cracked lips.

If truth be told, I think it was a mixture of things that put me on the road to recovery – counselling, medication, and just my life improving in general. Having a fulfilling job, our lovely kittens, and our beautiful home gave me a sense of contentment and safety I hadn't felt in a many years.

It took me a long time, and it was a hard road, but I got there. One of my best friends, Julie, bought me a beautiful honeycomb necklace to celebrate my last CBT session. It came with a little card that said "the harder the work, the sweeter the reward", and when I wear it, I'm reminded of the difficult and winding path I had to take to get me to where I am today.

Recovery isn't linear. There will be peaks and troughs, especially with OCD. I often found it was a case of "one step forward, ten steps back". I would stop doing one of my safety behaviours, but then another would spring up in its place like a thick, ugly weed. The irrational side of my brain was a master manipulator – it tricked, deceived, and bargained. It's hard to reason with the unreasonable.

I hit many walls during therapy. One of my tasks was to eat out-of-date food. I went shopping with my counsellor and bought a whole bag full of reduced items that were about to expire.

I managed a tiny bit of the cheesecake that was due to go out of date the next day, but I couldn't bring myself to eat any of the other items.

During one of my sessions, my counsellor tried to tackle my fear of touching food with unwashed hands.

She pointed to a packet of Mini Cheddars on her desk and asked me if I liked them.

'Yes ...' I answered warily.

'I want you to take one out of the bag.'

Slowly, I opened the bag and plucked out a Cheddar, careful to touch as little of it as possible.

'Do you think you could eat that now?'

My head almost fell off from how hard I was shaking it.

'Okay, then I'd like you to hold it in your hand for a bit and just focus on the sensation of it on your skin.'

So there I am, holding a Mini Cheddar in my hands, like it's the Holy fucking Grail, and wondering how long I'm going to have to sit there pretending I'm not feeling wildly uncomfortable.

'Do you think you could just rub it across your face?'

So now I'm slowly and almost sensually rubbing a cheesy biscuit on my face and, honestly, I'm starting to feel like I'm in a really weird, niche porno. I'd laugh if I didn't feel like such a twat.

'Start to get closer to your mouth ... there you go. Do you think you could run it across your lips?'

I mean, I can actually hear the "wah-wah" porno music.

I do as she's asked for a few moments, before ...

'Now do you think you could put it in your mouth?'

I'm a lady – if this bastard Mini Cheddar wants to get past third base, it's going to have to at least buy me dinner first.

And that's when it got even weirder. I know, not possible, right?

Oh yes, my friends. Oh yes.

My counsellor picked up the bag and took out another Mini Cheddar.

I watched the following things happen in horrified slow-mo:

- She rubbed it on the sole of her shoe.
- She put it on the floor and trod on it a bit more for good measure.
- She dropped to the floor on her hands and knees, brought her face to the Cheddar and ...
- *She licked it up. With her actual tongue. Off the actual floor.*

'How disgusted do you feel on a scale of one to ten?' she asked me once she'd polished off her carpet Ched.

I shuddered. Every fibre of my being roared with disgust and I wanted to scream that my capacity for revulsion had been maxed out. Somehow, I managed a nervous laugh instead.

Watching her do something so much worse than just touching her food with her fingers was supposed to give me some perspective. But rather than realising that my task wasn't so scary, I felt uneasy, grossed out, and fairly certain I'd never eat a Mini Cheddar again.

At the time I felt frustrated that I'd hit a wall with my exposure therapy. I hadn't lost faith in the process, but I'd lost faith in myself. In the sessions that followed, I diverted the focus onto other issues, in part because they felt more pressing, but also I suspect, deep down, because I didn't want to keep feeling like a failure.

My exposure therapy must have had more of an impact than I'd thought, as a mere matter of months later I accepted a sweet from a colleague. As I put my unwashed hand into the bag and popped the sweet straight into my mouth, I experienced some anxiety, but I breathed through it and it passed quickly. I felt so triumphant!

Gradually, my confidence grew. I ate food with my hands at work, trusted things like meat and prawns from the sandwich shop across the road from the office, and ate pre-packed salads again.

They were so lovely in there, and always accommodated my unusual requests, such as having my cake in a takeaway box with a fork. I was open about the fact that it was because I didn't feel comfortable touching it.

Eventually, though, I managed to graduate to having my cake in the same paper bag everyone else did. As the expression goes, I had my cake and ate it with my fingers too! Of course, I still wouldn't eat a Mini Cheddar off the floor, but I think that's reasonable, right?

I found it really helpful to look at others for guidance on how to do things. If I saw other people drinking out of cans without a care, or tucking into a chicken, bacon and avocado baguette from the sandwich shop, I kind of thought *ah, screw it* – they were doing it (and would be absolutely fine), so what was stopping me? And so, at an office party, I took a can of cider out of the fridge, opened it and drank directly from the can, not concerned about the other fingers that might have touched it. Maybe watching others is a form of reassurance seeking, I don't know. But it really helps me.

Counselling taught me a lot of things. I learnt a lot about myself and developed better coping strategies. But most importantly, I learnt that you're never really fully prepared to see a grown woman lick a Mini Cheddar off the floor like a cat.

I've learnt that telling others what I need isn't selfish. That my views, thoughts, and beliefs are valid. That it's okay to step away from situations that I can't handle. I've learnt that I matter.

For so long, OCD made me an expert at justifying my behaviour – not just to others, but also to myself.

That's just how I wash my hands; there's nothing wrong with being clean.

So I say certain words in a specific order? It's not hurting anyone.

That was, perhaps, the biggest lie of all, because it was hurting me. As soon as each ritual came to end, all the panic and frustration I felt magically evaporated. These moments became blips, or "wobblies" as I used to call them. The rest of the time, I reasoned, I was completely fine. Until the next night when I'd be lying in bed, counting to 100 again. I became very good at tricking myself and stretching the wool I'd pulled over other people's eyes over my own as well.

That, I think, is another cruel difference between mental illness and physical pain.

For all the dark times I've faced, however, my mental illness has given me a few laughs as well. When you wash your hands as thoroughly as I do, you tend to get a few comments from other people – 'What time are you due in surgery?', 'Out, out, damn spot!' etc. etc. – but my all-time favourite was this masterpiece of creepiness from a former colleague.

He came up behind me while I was washing my hands in the kitchen at work and said, 'You look like you're washing away your sins.'

I laughed, nervously.

Then he said, 'You must have a *lot* of sins.'

As he walked away, I questioned whether he would one day murder me, but it still makes me laugh when I think about it.

I believe that finding humour where we can is a great way to cope. I call my sertraline "Pilbert" and my propranolol "Mega

Propranololz". Instead of these scary tablets, they've become characters in my life who are there to help me.

I make jokes, not to trivialise my struggles, or belittle others', but to find levity in otherwise shitty situations.

I'm known among my friends as a serial blocker of toilets, due to my propensity to use more loo roll than is necessary. I'm not so bad anymore (in fact, it's been over a year since my last incident), but one of the ways my OCD used to loom over me was toilet-time cleanliness.

One time I blocked my friend's loo (in my defence, it clogs easily – lesser men than I have succeeded at blocking that thing) and by way of apology I sent a bunch of flowers to her workplace with a card that read:

"Roses are red,
Violets are blue
I'm ever so sorry
For blocking your loo."

It made us both giggle, and is just one example of the ways I feel perfectly comfortable making a tit of myself and laughing at the ridiculous situations my OCD puts me in.

I've got to a point now where I still have wobbles, but my life isn't controlled by OCD anymore. My fears are still there lingering in the background, but they by no means stop me from doing the things I want to do. I have doubts in myself, like most people do, but I know my worth, and I believe in myself again. I respect myself enough to know that my feelings are just as valid as anyone else's, and to assert myself if necessary.

I say yes to opportunities and enjoy socialising and being out in the world again. I laugh, I feel joy, I look forward to things, and I feel genuine excitement about the future – something that the apathetic, exhausted husk of a person I was in 2016 couldn't possibly have imagined.

I've also learnt that I don't need to understand *everything*. One of my goals in counselling was to better understand myself and why I think and do things the way I do. I achieved this goal, insofar as I gained a better understanding of how my past trauma helped to shape me as a person, and where a lot of my insecurities come from.

But there are also many things I will probably never get to the bottom of. I'll likely never truly understand why my parents treated me the way they did. I remember my counsellor asking me, 'But why does that actually matter?' and I guess she was right. Some things don't need understanding; they just *are*. It doesn't benefit me at all to ruminate on what happened or make speculations, so I've reached a point of acceptance about what happened. Rather than being stuck in the past, I'm moving forward, and it feels good.

I've channelled my experiences into doing little things to give others hope. In sharing my story and being candid online, I hope to help other people feel less alone. Where I can, I try to start conversations about mental health, and do my part to help dispel myth and shatter stigma.

When a good friend (Danny, the mopper of blood, for context!) sent me a "get well soon" card during a dark period, it struck me that while the gesture was incredibly thoughtful, the sentiment of the card wasn't quite right. I wasn't necessarily going to "get better" in the same way one recovers from a cold. Recovery from mental illness isn't as linear, or as measurable. Plus, it can take time.

This inspired me to create Honey Bee Cards, a range of cards that say all the words I'd like to have heard. They are reminders that it's okay to not be okay, reminders that we are so much more than the things we tell ourselves in our darkest moments, and reminders that we are not alone.

"It's OK if you don't feel like hanging out right now.

I'm here when you need me.

But, if I don't hear from you in a while I may pop round to check you haven't been eaten by a bear ..."

"You are loved.

You are strong.

You are beautiful.

You are amazing.

You are not what you think you are in your darkest hours."

"Do what you need to do.

Cry. Sleep. Shout.

I'm here for whatever you need.

(And I've got a great pair of lungs!)"

"It's OK if you're struggling right now.

Never be afraid to tell me what you need.

Even if it's just a hug and a shepherd's pie."

The messages are sweet, silly, and most importantly, human. They're written in the same way you'd talk to a mate, rather than the stiff, formal language of a generic "get well soon" card. I've had wonderful feedback from people who've said the words were exactly what they needed to hear, and who were truly touched by their meaning.

Recently, I decided to get a tattoo. I wanted something symbolic and special to me that represented my strength and courage. I loved the concept of the semicolon tattoo. The meaning behind Project Semicolon felt so fitting – a semicolon is used when the author could end their sentence, but chooses not to.

However, the night before I was supposed to get it, I started to have second thoughts. Something about it didn't feel quite right. I'd never been close to ending my life and it felt wrong to suggest otherwise. Everyone would see it and make assumptions about what I've been through. And those assumptions would be wrong.

At about two o'clock in the morning I was poogling tattoo ideas. A while back I'd tweeted asking for ideas for a *Gilmore Girls*-inspired tattoo, and one of the suggestions had been a dragonfly, as a nod to Lorelai's inn. I'd dismissed the idea as it didn't feel very "me", but on a whim I Googled dragonflies and what they symbolise.

I found out that they symbolise courage, power, and poise. They represent the kind of self-realisation that stems from mental and emotional maturity. They also represent change and strength through adversity. In their own way they shared a similar meaning to the semicolon, with the added bonus of being a nice little nod to *Gilmore Girls*.

Writing this book has been such a surreal experience. I've known for a long time that I had a story in me that was waiting to be told; I just thought it would be one about a fictional land of myth and magic – I never dreamt it would be my own.

I still dream of one day writing that work of fiction, but for now let me just say that it's been an honour and a joy to share my story with you.

All my life I've been desperate to know who I am, and find a sense of belonging. After a long struggle, I finally feel like I'm there. I have a home and a close network of friends and family. I know what my passions are and what I have to offer. I have a new-found assertiveness and a voice that CBT helped me to find.

I've found a man I love with all my heart and, at the end of 2017, we (along with Marty and Plum of course!) moved out of our flat and into our beautiful new home.

I can't put into words how happy it makes me spending time with my gorgeous little family, in our very own little house. When we're all cosy on the sofa with the cats snoozing next to us, or having our Sunday morning coffee in bed and Marty and Plum jump up and have a snuggle with us, I feel like the luckiest person in the whole world.

Sometimes I'll look around, whether I'm at home, laughing and joking with Dave's family, or surrounded by my friends, and I can't believe how fortunate I am. I've found my place in the world and the people I want to share it with. I'm still super close to my two best friends. And you remember Pete, our housemate a few years back? He ended up married to Julie! So, Dave's best friend married my best friend, and our houses are just two streets away from each other. We've been each other's bridesmaids and best men, holidayed together, been there for each other through highs and lows, and laughed until our sides hurt. They really are family to us.

I'm so thankful for all the friends I've made along the way: the friends I met at university, the amazing people who've come into my life since I moved to Bournemouth, and the online friends who have quickly become IRL friends. I'm grateful to have each and every one of you.

Our new home afforded us a fresh start on so many other levels, too. We'd been in our flat for seven years and accumulated quite a lot of stuff. I made it my mission to clear everything out – I was *brutal*. I wanted our new home to be filled only with things we loved and wanted.

When we got the keys, we worked hard every weekend and most evenings after work to paint and decorate everything how we wanted. We got new carpets and furniture, fought over curtains, and set everything up exactly how we liked. We have this really cute little nook under the stairs that I fell in love with the first time I viewed the house, and I turned it into a cosy space filled with cushions and fairy lights.

It felt like the cleanest, freshest of starts, and I couldn't have predicted just how much I love our home.

The postman and pizza delivery guy can actually find our house, and I no longer have to walk down Shit Alley to get to the front door. With mostly hard floors downstairs making for super easy cleaning, and a dishwasher and all-new kitchen appliances, I not only love cleaning now, but I enjoy and trust cooking in our kitchen again. Since I had hated our kitchen in the flat, and because we only had a tiny dining table, mealtimes simply served a purpose, rather than being something I looked forward to and enjoyed. Now, however, I love cooking and hosting, and eating our meals at the dining table.

In the flat, the bathroom was also one of my difficult areas.

Now though, our bathroom is lovely and fresh and spacious, which has massively helped with my need for showering every time I use the toilet. And by that I mean, I don't "need" to do it anymore. I've gone from maybe eight showers a day to a much more reasonable morning and night-time shower.

Perhaps my biggest achievement is that I no longer "need" my "decontamination showers". Remember the goal I made with my second counsellor? To be able to come home and sit on the sofa, or potter round the kitchen without needing to shower? That's just standard for me now. I don't feel dirty all the time – not only do I feel more comfortable in my own house, but I feel more comfortable in my own skin too.

Home really is my happy place now, my haven from the outside world – a place where I can well and truly feel relaxed. This feels huge, when it was something I feared I'd never have again.

If you know someone who's struggling, I hope my experiences have given you bit of insight into how you can help support them. If you're the one who's struggling, I'm here to remind you that things can and *will* get better. There is help available and you deserve to reach out and ask for it.

All my life I longed for stability, home, family, and a sense of belonging. I finally feel like I have all those things. I finally feel happy. I've found acceptance of who I am and the confidence to share that openly.

As weird as this may sound, I wouldn't change any of my experiences. It's thanks to my mental illness that I know how resilient I am. It showed me what I can endure and that I have the strength to fight my way to a point where I'm no longer just surviving. I've seen that no matter how exhausted or hopeless I've felt, I've never quite lost that little spark of fight within me.

Thank you. Thank you to my past, my illness, and the fear that's haunted me for so many years.

Thank you for showing me what I'm made of.

ACKNOWLEDGEMENTS

First and foremost, I'd like to thank Trigger Publishing, without whom this book wouldn't exist. Thank you for finding my blog, and for seeing in me a story I didn't realise I had. Thanks especially to Katie and my wonderful editor, Stephanie. A huge thank you for reassuring me that I wasn't writing what I often called a "pile of wank". And of course, for taking my rambles and somehow turning them into a book; yours is a special kind of magic.

Thank you to my wonderful friends – you know who you are. I truly believe that friends are the family you choose for yourself, and I have to say, I've chosen well.

And now, my husband, because I guess you probably deserve a mention. I don't have the words to fully express how thankful I am that we found each other. You are without a doubt the kindest, most supportive and wonderful man I could have hoped to meet. You make me happy every day, and your special brand of silliness never fails to make me laugh. You'll be just across the kitchen table, always.

Thank you to our cats, Marty and Plum, for your invaluable help chewing on the corners of my manuscript. I couldn't have done it without you.

I'm so grateful to all the strong, courageous people who make up the online mental health community. Without you, this book may not have happened. Keep sharing your stories. Your voices are helping to change the world, and I hope you remember that whenever you feel like giving up.

Lastly, I want to say an enormous thank you to my family. To those who are still with us – and those who sadly aren't – I hope I make you proud.

**If you found this book interesting ...
why not read these next?**

Depression in a Digital Age

The Highs and Lows of Perfectionism

Depression in a Digital Age traces the journey of a young woman's search for perfection in a world filled with filters.

Every Trich in the Book

Overcoming My Hair Pulling Disorder

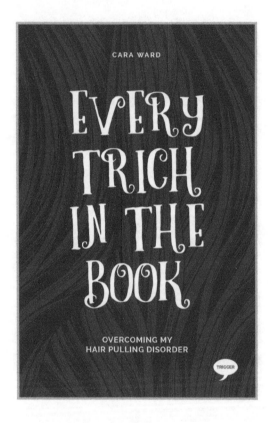

Through sheer determination, Cara found a way to get to the best place she'd ever been with her trichotillomania, a condition that had left her scarred and ashamed for years.

A Series of Unfortunate Stereotypes

Naming and Shaming Mental Health Stigmas

Drawing on her personal experience with anxiety, Lucy tackles a number of different stereotypes placed on people living with mental illness with wicked humour and a dose of 80s sparkle.

A Series of Unfortunate Stereotypes

Naming and Shaming Mental Health Stigma

the *Shaw* mind
FOUNDATION

Creating hope for children,
adults and families

Sign up to our charity, The Shaw Mind Foundation

www.shawmindfoundation.org

and keep in touch with us; we would love to hear
from you.

*We aim to bring to an end the suffering and despair caused
by mental health issues. Our goal is to make help and support
available for every single person in society, from all walks of
life. We will never stop offering hope. These are our promises.*

www.triggerpublishing.com

Trigger is a publishing house devoted to opening conversations about mental health. We tell the stories of people who have suffered from mental illnesses and recovered, so that others may learn from them.

Adam Shaw is a worldwide mental health advocate and philanthropist. Now in recovery from mental health issues, he is committed to helping others suffering from debilitating mental health issues through the global charity he co-founded, The Shaw Mind Foundation. www.shawmindfoundation.org

Lauren Callaghan (CPsychol, PGDipClinPsych, PgCert, MA (hons), LLB (hons), BA), born and educated in New Zealand, is an innovative industry-leading psychologist based in London, United Kingdom. Lauren has worked with children and young people, and their families, in a number of clinical settings providing evidence based treatments for a range of illnesses, including anxiety and obsessional problems. She was a psychologist at the specialist national treatment centres for severe obsessional problems in the UK and is renowned as an expert in the field of mental health, recognised for diagnosing and successfully treating OCD and anxiety related illnesses in particular. In addition to appearing as a treating clinician in the critically acclaimed and BAFTA award-winning documentary *Bedlam*, Lauren is a frequent guest speaker on mental health conditions in the media and at academic conferences. Lauren also acts as a guest lecturer and honorary researcher at the Institute of Psychiatry Kings College, UCL.

Please visit the link below:

www.triggerpublishing.com

Join us and follow us...

@triggerpub

Search for us on Facebook